India Tourist Cities
Agra, Delhi, Jaipur Travel Guide.

Author
Caleb Gray.

SONITTEC PUBLISHING. All rights reserved. No part of this publication may be reproduced, distributed, or transmitted in any form or by any means, including photocopying, recording, or other electronic or mechanical methods, without the prior written permission of the publisher, except in the case of brief quotations embodied in critical reviews and certain other noncommercial uses permitted by copyright law. For permission requests, write to the publisher, addressed "Attention: Permissions Coordinator," at the address below.

Copyright © 2019 Sonittec Publishing
All Rights Reserved

First Printed: 2019.

Publisher:
SONITTEC LTD
College House, 2nd Floor
17 King Edwards Road,
Ruislip
London
HA4 7AE

Table of Content

- **SUMMARY** 1
- **INTRODUCTION** 4
- **INDIA CITIES INFORMATION** 8
  - AGRA 8
    - History of Agra 8
    - Things to Do in Agra 10
      - Agra Tourist Attractions 10
        - Taj Mahal 12
        - Agra Red Fort 16
        - Fatehpur Sikri 18
        - Buland Darwaza 20
        - Jama Masjid 22
        - Tomb of Itimad Ud Daulah 24
        - Taj Mahal Museum 26
        - Akbar's Tomb at Sikandra 28
        - Moti Masjid 30
        - Taj Mahal Garden 31
        - Shah Jahan Park 33
        - Spiritual Museum 35
        - Ram Bagh 37
        - Mehtab Bagh 39
        - Mangleshwar Temple 41
        - Dayalbagh Gardens 42
        - Chini ka Rauza 44
        - Bageshwarnath Temple 46
        - Guru Ka Taal 47
    - Best Time to Visit Agra 51
    - How to Reach in Agra 52
    - Monuments in Agra 54
    - Agra Excursions 56
    - Gardens in Agra 58
    - Shopping in Agra 60
      - Bazaars in Agra 62
    - Fairs and Festivals in Agra 64
  - DELHI 67
    - History of New Delhi 67
    - Things to Do in New Delhi 69
      - Delhi Tourist Attractions 69
        - Red Fort 70
        - India Gate 74
        - Humayun's Tomb 80
        - ISKCON Temple 82

    Qutab Minar 86
    Purana Qila - Old Fort 89
    Buddha Jayanti Park 96
    National Science Center 99
    Nizamuddin's Tomb 104
    Parliament House 111
    Delhi Zoo 117
    Railway Museum 122
    Rajghat in Delhi... 124
    Rashtrapati Bhavan 132
    Safdarjung's Tomb 136
    Jama Masjid 143
    Lakshmi Narayan Temple 151
    Metro Walk Rohini 156
    Meena Bazaar.. 160
    Lodi Gardens 163
    Deer Park in New Delhi 170
    Gurdwara Bangla Sahib in Delhi 173
    Jantar Mantar 179
Best Time to Visit New Delhi 184
Monuments in Delhi 185
Memorials in Delhi 186
Where to Go 189
    Gurgaon Gurgaon 191
Best Time to Visit New Delhi 193
Museums in Delhi 195
Parks and Gardens in Delhi 198
    Deer Park in New Delhi 198
    Garden of Five Senses 202
    Talkatora Garden 207
    National Rose Garden 212
    Buddha Jayanti Park 215
    Lodi Gardens 218
    Mughal Garden 226
Restaurants in New Delhi 229
Shopping in New Delhi 230
Entertainment in New Delhi 232
Weather in New Delhi 234
Fairs and Festivals in Delhi 235
JAIPUR 236
  History of Jaipur 237
  Economy of Jaipur 240
  Culture of Jaipur 243
  Festivals in Jaipur 249
  Famous Jaipuri Print 253

- Nightlife in Jaipur 255
- Lifestyle in Jaipur 258
- Shopping in Jaipur 261
- Public Transport in Jaipur 267
    - Jaipur Airport 273
    - Jaipur Metro 279
    - Jaipur Railway Station 282
    - Trains from Jaipur 284

Summary

The importance of travelling in our life?
Everyone has their very own reasons to travel. Some people travel for work, some travel for pleasure while for others it is just a way of life. They travel to live and to escape at the same time.

Whatever might be the reason to travel, here are few ways in which travelling would definitely change you and I think that is why travelling becomes so important in life:

Enjoy being alone: There is something therapeutic about being alone and being at peace with it. While you soak in a new culture, you also connect with your own inner self.

Learn to adapt: It is a different world out there, literally. Be it the pace of life, the language or simply the change in weather, it is always a change and you have to adapt to it. This is what makes travelling truly beautiful as you break away from the routine and adapt to something totally new.

Experience a new culture: Every place comes with its distinct cultural habits, you cannot think about New York without talking about its fast paced life and about Italy without enjoying its relaxed lifestyle. Similarly, while visiting the UK you might have to be a bit formal in your interactions with the locals, on the other hand, while greeting the people in Thailand, one can be really warm and casual.

Broaden your taste buds: Travelling without experiencing the local food is just not complete. It is not only a culinary experience but a cultural one as well.

Get out of comfort zone: From simple experiences like the weather, way of life or food to the more adventurous ones like trying a new sport, travelling really pushes ones boundaries to the core. You might end up participating in a street carnival in Brazil just like the locals or trying the local delicacies (read insects) in Thailand.

Indulge in Photography: It does not matter whether you are a professional or not. It is also irrelevant whether you have a DSLR or a very basic camera, while travelling what matters is the love and quest for seeing beautiful places and the sheer joy of capturing them in your lense. Travelling would in return give you your very own collection of amazing postcards of beautiful sunsets, snow laced mountains or sunny beaches.

Learn to escape: Travelling is the best way to break the routine. If you are in a bustling city, go ahead and experience the country life. If you are in a rural place, travel to a bustling city and experience its madness. Stressed with the city life or work pressure? A spa break in Himalayas or Kerala is a must try.

Appreciate Nature: The quest to explore more when one is travelling always leads to a sense of amazement about nature. While most of us keep a track of technological advancements, Nature has its own ways of outshining all of these. The Antelope Canyon in Arizona or Turquoise Ice in Russia are the finest examples of this. For more, check out the most unbelievable places around the world.

Get closer to your own roots: While one travels and experiences a lot of different cultures and practices, it definitely brings one closer to his or her own roots. Travel helps one appreciate one's identity and culture.

Travelling is all about experiences. They can happen in terms of culture, people, places but most importantly with one's own self and this was all about

Introduction

So far as I am able to judge, nothing has been left undone, either by man or nature, to make India the most extraordinary country that the sun visits on his rounds. Nothing seems to have been forgotten, nothing overlooked." --Mark Twain, from Following the Equator

It is impossible not to be astonished by India. Nowhere on Earth does humanity present itself in such a dizzying, creative burst of cultures and religions, races and tongues. Every aspect of the country presents itself on a massive, exaggerated scale, worthy in comparison only to the superlative mountains that overshadow it. Perhaps the only thing more difficult than to be indifferent to India would be to describe or understand India completely.

India Set apart from the rest of Asia by the supreme continental wall of the Himalayas, the Indian subcontinent touches three large bodies of water and is immediately recognizable on any world map. It is the huge, terrestrial beak between Africa and Indonesia. This thick, roughly triangular peninsula defines the

Bay of Bengal to the east, the Arabian sea to the west, and the India Ocean to the south.

India's puzzleboard of 26 states holds virtually every kind of landscape imaginable. An abundance of mountain ranges and national parks provide ample opportunity for eco-tourism and trekking, and its sheer size promises something for everyone. From its northernmost point on the Chinese border, India extends a good 2000 miles (3200 km) to its southern tip, where the island nation of Sri Lanka seems to be squeezed out of India like a great tear, the synapse forming the Gulf of Mannar. India's northern border is dominated mostly by Nepal and the Himalayas, the world's highest mountain chain. Following the sweeping mountains to the northeast, its borders narrow to a small channel that passes between Nepal, Tibet, Bangladesh, and Bhutan, then spreads out again to meet Burma in area called the "eastern triangle." Apart from the Arabian sea, its western border is defined exclusively by Pakistan.

India can be organized along the compass points. North India, shaped like a throat and two lungs, is the country's largest region. It begins with the panhandle of Jammu and Kashmir, a dynamic area with terrain varying from arid mountains in the far north to the lake country and forests near Sringar and Jammu. Falling south along the Indus river valley, the North becomes flatter and more hospitable, widening into the fertile plains of Punjab to the west and the Himalayan foothills of Uttar Pradesh and the Ganges river valley to the East. Cramped between these two states is the capital city, Delhi. The southwestern extremity of the North is the large state of Rajastan, whose principal features are the Thar Desert and the stunning "pink city" of Jaipur. To the southeast is southern Uttar Pradesh and Agra, home of the famous Taj Mahal.

West India contains the states of Gujarat, Maharashtra, Goa, and part of the massive, central state of Madhya Pradesh. The west coast extends from the Gujarat peninsula down to Goa, and it is lined with some of India's best beaches. The land along the coast is typically lush, with rainforests reaching southward from Bombay all the way to into Goa. A long mountain chain, the Western Ghats, separates the verdant coast from the Vindya mountains and the dry Deccan plateau further inland.

Home of the sacred Ganges river and the majority of Himalayan foothills, East India begins with the states of Madhya Pradesh, Bihar, Orissa, which comprise the westernmost part of the region. East India also contains an area known as the eastern triangle, which is entirely distinct. This is the last gulp of land that extends beyond Bangladesh, culminating in the Naga Hills along the Burmese border.

India reaches its peninsular tip with South India, which begins with the Deccan in the north and ends with Cape Comorin, where Hindus believe that bathing in the waters of the three oceans will wash away their sins. The states in South India are Karnataka, Andhra Pradesh, Tamil Nadu, and Kerala, a favorite leisure destination. The southeast coast, mirroring the west, also rests snugly beneath a mountain range---the Eastern Ghats.

Because of India's size, its climate depends not only on the time of year, but also the location. In general, temperatures tend to be cooler in the north, especially between September and March. The south is coolest between November to January. In June, winds and warm surface currents begin to move northwards and westwards, heading out of the Indian Ocean and into the Arabian Gulf. This creates a phenomenon known as the south-west monsoon, and it brings heavy rains to the west coast. Between October and December, a similar climatic pattern called the north-east monsoon appears in the Bay of Bengal, bringing rains to the east coast. In addition to the two monsoons, there are two other seasons, spring and autumn.

Though the word "monsoon" often brings to mind images of torrential floods and landslides, the monsoon seasons are not bad times to come to India. Though it rains nearly every day, the downpour tends to come and go quickly, leaving behind a clean, glistening landscape.

With nearly 1 billion citizens, India is the second most populous nation in the world. It is impossible to speak of any one Indian culture, although there are deep cultural continuities that tie its people together. English is the major language of trade and politics, but there are fourteen official languages in all. There are twenty-four languages that are spoken by a million people or more, and countless other dialects. India has seven major religions and many minor ones, six main ethnic groups, and countless holidays.

Religion is central to Indian culture, and its practice can be seen in virtually every aspect of life in the country. Hinduism is the dominant faith of India, serving about 80 percent of the population. Ten percent worship Islam, and 5 perscent are Sikhs and Christians; the rest (a good 45 million) are Buddhists, Jains, Bahai, and more

India Cities Information

Agra

History of Agra

History of Agra has quite a rich background, which is fully apparent from the various historical monuments that are located in and around the city. The initial reference for the city of Agra comes from the age of epic, when in the Mahabharata Agra was referred to as "Agravana". Agra has also been referred to as "Arya Griha" which means the abode of the Aryans. There has been a lot of historical influence on this lovely city and the Agra's history gets reverberated in the historical monuments that have been built during the rule of the Mughals.

Not only the Mughals, there were a lot of other rulers who were responsible for the rich heritage and history of Agra. The one who was responsible for finding the city of Agra was Sikandar Lodhi who belonged to the lodhi dynasty of the Delhi Sultanate and it was in the 16th century. One could notice the square Persian-styled gardens which were for the first time introduced by another Mughal emperor Babar. The History of Agra city witnessed another gem being added to its crown when Emperor Akbar first built the Agra fort and Fatehpur Sikri close to Agra.

Under the bizarre circumstances Fatehpur Sikri got demolished and was left isolated that had remained the capital of Akbar for a long span of fifteen years. History of Agra has witnessed a lot of things being added and removed to it and hence has a rich past that simply captivates the tourists when spoken about. The beautification of Agra city was done by Jahangir with splendid palaces and verdant gardens. The actual beautification was done when Shajahan ascended the throne of the Mughal Empire and built the famous Taj Mahal in the memory of his beloved wife Mumtaz Mahal.

In the later stage of his life he shifted to Shahjahanabad and ruled from there itself.

It was after the death of Aurangzeb that the history of Agra saw the emergence of many small kingdoms such as Jats, Marathas and lastly the British Empire taking over the city.

Things to Do in Agra

Agra Tourist Attractions

Situated on the banks of the Yamuna River, Agra is known for its rich culture and Mughal heritage. It was the Mughal capital from 1526 to 1658 and the emperors built majestic forts and monuments during their reign here. Taj Mahal, the undying symbol of love, makes Agra an unrivaled tourist destination. This marvel is at the zenith of Mughal architectural splendor. Agra tourist attractions are the reason why the domestic and international travelers throng this city throughout the year.

Popular Agra tourist attractions

Check out the famous tourist sites in Agra city.

Taj Mahal: This is undoubtedly the most beautiful mausoleum in the country. It was built by Mughal Emperor Shah Jahan in the memory of his wife Mumtaz Mahal. Impressive features of this white marble monument include its fine blend of Central Asian, Persian, and Islamic architecture. Designed by a Persian architect Ustad Isa, the construction of this monument took 20,000 men and 22 years! Its majestic dome measures 213 feet in height and its interiors were in-laid with semi precious stones. The four minarets resemble those of a mosque which is integral to the Islamic style of architecture.

Agra Fort: Within minutes of the Taj Mahal stands the historic Agra Fort, another UNESCO World Heritage Sites in Agra city. This red sand stone complex was initiated by Mughal Emperor Akbar. Jehangir and Shah Jahan later added mosques and other structures in this fort complex. Tourist attractions here include the Moti Masjid or the Pearl Mosque, Shish Mahal (palace of glass) and the Nagina Masjid (gem mosque). You can also visit the Diwan-i-Aam and Musamman Burj.

Fatehpur Sikri: This third World Heritage Site in Agra is located around 35 km from the main city. It was the capital of Mughal Emperor Akbar from 1591 to 1585. It has a blend of Indo-Islamic architecture with the Buland Darwaza being its prime attraction. Towering 54 meters in height, it is the largest gateway to any monument in the world. Fatehpur Sikri has the tomb of Shaikh Salim Chisti, a famous Sufi saint.

Itimad-Ud-Daulah: Mughal Empress Nur Jahan built this tomb in memory of her father, Mirza Ghiyas Beg. Situated on the left bank of Yamuna River, it is among the popular Agra tourist attractions. The main mausoleum covers 24 square meters of area and is built on a raised platform. The white marble for construction was brought from Rajasthan and its interiors have images of trees, fruits and vases.

Other important landmarks in Agra include Akbar's Tomb at Sikandra, Jama Masjid, Chini Ka Rauza, and Ram Bagh.

Taj Mahal

Taj Mahal, a universally admired UNESCO World Heritage Site, is a monument epitomizing love of the Mughal Emperor Shah Jahan for his wife Mumtaz. Taj Mahal is regarded as one of the eight wonders of the world.

Some Western historians also define it as a monument whose architectural beauty has never been surpassed by many others. Taj Mahal is the most beautiful monument built by the Mughals in India and also the most important tourist attraction in Agra. Made up of white marble, its astonishing architectural beauty is beyond any description. Located by the river of Yamuna in Agra, it is believed to glow in the light of the full moon. It is on the full moon day that the monument sees accumulation of huge crowds to witness its serene look. On a winter morning, when the Taj is shrouded by fog, it appears to be suspended in mid-air, thereby surprising the visitors to no end.

Taj Mahal in Agra stands on top of a red sandstone base on which lies the huge white marble terrace. On the white marbled terrace rests the famous dome bordered by four tapering minarets. Within the dome like structure lies the jewel-inlaid cenotaph of the queen named Mumtaz. The Taj that is the casket of the emperor was built beside the queen's one as an afterthought. The emperor was once overthrown by his son and imprisoned in the Great Red Fort for eight years before being finally buried in the Taj Mahal.

History of Taj Mahal Agra

The history of Taj Mahal has been an interesting topic of research and study for a long time. Many a travelers, after visiting this fabulous structure, look for the story behind its construction. It was built by Mughal Emperor Shah Jahan in memory of his beloved queen, Mumtaz.

Emperor Shah Jahan was the ruler from 1628 to 1658, and within his lifetime, he built the tomb for his wife Mumtaz Mahal. Shah Jahan got married to beautiful Arjumand Bano Begum in 1612 A.D. He called his beloved wife Mumtaz Mahal as he wanted to refer to her as the crown of the Palace as she was so precious to him. This royal couple had 14 children. The queen used to accompany Emperor Shah Jahan everywhere, even on military campaigns and in one such campaign in Burhanpur in central India, Mumtaz Mahal died in 1631 shortly after giving birth to her 14th child.

It was Mumtaz's dying wish to Shah Jahan that he should build a tomb in her memory. She mentioned it specifically that the tomb should be such that world had never seen something of that sort before. Shah Jahan fulfilled her last wish and created the most beautiful mausoleum in the world. Taj Mahal was completed with a consistent effort of 22 long years. A huge labor force of 20,000 workers worked regularly led by Muhammed Hanif, the head of the masons. The Persian architect Ustad Isa designed the great tomb, which ultimately cost the Mughal exchequer 32 million rupees.

In later years of his life, Shah Jahan was ousted by his son Aurangzeb. The lonely emperor spent the last years of his life under house arrest in the Agra Fort from where he made an arrangement to spend his time looking at the beautiful tomb he had built for his beloved empress and waited patiently for the day they could be united again. After Shah Jahan's death in 1666 A.D., he too was buried beside his beloved Mumtaz Mahal.

Architecture of Taj Mahal Agra

Architecture of Taj Mahal has been praised by the whole world for its innovative talents. It's been more than 350 years now, but still the glorious tomb has not lost its glory with time. Persian architect Ustad Isa designed the great tomb called Taj Mahal in Agra and received the world acclaim for his ingenuity. The Taj Mahal had cost the Mughal exchequer 32 million rupees and took 22 years to be constructed. It was Mumtaz's, the empresses' dying wish to Shah Jahan that he should build a tomb in her memory. She mentioned it specifically that the tomb should be such that world had never seen something of that sort before. Shah Jahan fulfilled her last wish and created the most beautiful mausoleum of the world.

Architecturally, Taj Mahal was the greatest of all the architectural works of the Mughals. It is far superior to any of the monuments in India in the pride of its grouping and character. The Taj Mahal Agra has a rare contrast of temperament and order between the central dome and the slender minarets. Taj Mahal shows the perfection done in the pure form of refinement. The painstaking craftsmanship with its intricate details speaks about the splendor and aura of love that is embedded in its every corner. The design of Taj is believed to be more Persian and less Indian. But in the heart of hearts it is completely original and inimitable.

Agra Red Fort

Agra Fort is a World Heritage Site that captivates the onlooker at first sight with its colossal dimensions and stately aura. The majestic fort is located in the beautiful Indian city of Agra in Uttar Pradesh. Its premises contain a number of exquisite buildings like Moti Masjid, Diwan-i-Aam, Diwan-i-Khas and Musamman Burj, where Shah Jahan died in imprisonment. Some of the other important monuments inside the Fort are Jahangir's Palace, Khaas Mahal and Sheesh Mahal.

Known to many as Red Fort of Agra or Fort Rouge owing to the lavish use of red sandstone, the enclosure houses several sites and structures that display royal Mughal architectural heritage and splendor. Some of the exquisite structures that deserve a mention are:

<u>Sheesh Mahal</u> - Literally meaning 'Glass Palace', it was the royal dressing room adorned by tiny mirror-like glass-mosaic decorations on the walls.

Diwan-i-Aam - This was used as a communications ground between the public and the aristocracy and once housed the Peacock Throne.

Diwan-i-Khas - A hall of private audience, it was used to welcome kings and dignitaries.

Anguri Bagh – Built in Shah Jahan in 1637, Anguri Bagh, flanked by Khas Mahal on the east and red sandstones on the remaining three sides, this garden served as a private area of relaxation for the royal ladies. The garden is divided into various subdivisions with elaborate geometric patterns.

Khas Mahal - Khas Mahal, also known as Aramgah-i-Muqaddar, was a private palace built by Shah Jahan for his daughters Roshanara and Jahanara. It consists of heavily adorned ceilings and alcoves in the surrounding walls. The interiors of the palace captivate the onlookers with gold work, mural paintings, ornamental and floral designs.

Mina Masjid - Literally meaning 'Heavenly Mosque', it is a tiny mosque closed to the public. Built between 1631-40, this mosque was meant to be used by the emperor and the royal ladies. Enclosed on all sides by three walls, its architecture is quite plain yet elegant.

<u>Nagina Masjid</u> - Literally meaning 'Gem Mosque', it was designed exclusively for the ladies of the court.

<u>Musamman Burj</u> – Musamman Burg, or the Octagonal Tower, is believed to have been built by Shah Jahan as the palace of his beloved queen, Mumtaz Mahal. It was here that he spent his last days as his son Aurangzeb imprisoned him till his death along with his favorite daughter, Jahanara Begum. It offers exotic views of the Taj.

Fatehpur Sikri

Fatehpur Sikri, a UNESCO World Heritage Site in Agra, along with its adjoining areas, are home to some of the finest examples of Mughal architecture and showcase one of the most brilliant phases of Indian history. One of these is Fatehpur Sikri, one of the best examples of Mughal planning and architecture. One of the most important aspects of Fatehpur Sikri is the fact that it provides us with details of not just Mughal architecture but paints an accurate image of the system of administration and social structure of the era. Once the political capital of Akbar, believed to be the greatest Mughal emperor, Fatehpur Sikri was in operation from 1571 to1585. Today a world heritage site, this erstwhile capital of the Mughals is a historian's delight and must-see for all visitors to the area.

History

Located on the outskirts of Agra, at a distance of only 26 miles, Fatehpur Sikri was one of the most important bases of Mughal rule and the capital of Akbar during 1571 to 1585. Fatehpur Sikri was instrumental in being one of the places along with Agra and Red Fort, where a bulk of the Mughal arsenal, treasure hoards and other reserves were stored. Legend has it that the fort was built as a tribute to the great Sufi Saint Sheikh Salim Chishti, with whose blessing Prince Salim, Akbar's descendent, was born.

Architecture

Built predominantly of red sandstone, Fatehpur Sikri is one of the earliest planned cities in the world. The layout of the city is in itself a work of architectural brilliance where a conscious effort has been made to produce rich spatial effects. On the other hand, the cityscape changes rapidly as we move across it indicating important buildings and also allowing these important localities to form a backdrop to other localities.

Main attractions

- ➢ Naubat Khana

- Diwan-i-Am
- Diwan-i-Khas
- Raja Birbal's house
- Joda Bai's House
- Pachisi Court
- Char Chaman Tank
- Panch Mahal
- Buland Darwaza
- Jama Masjid
- Tomb of Salim Chisti
- Jama Masjid

Buland Darwaza

Agra is well-known as being home to the wonderful Taj Mahal - one of the Seven Wonders of the World. The gracefully designed mausoleums, the fort and the palaces reminds of the Mughal architectural brilliance. Besides the Taj Mahal, other popular tourist spots in Agra are the Agra Fort, Jama Masjid, Itmad-Ud-Daulah's Tomb, Chini Ka Rauza, Rambagh Gardens, Fatehpur Sikri, etc. One such tourist attraction in Agra is the Buland Darwaza , a grand gateway located in Fatehpur Sikri near Agra.

Background

The Buland Darwaza is the entrance gateway to the Jama Masjid mosque in Fatehpur Sikri near Agra. It is situated on a hill where the Mosque is located. The grand recessed central arch is the most magnificent of its kind in the entire range of Mughal architecture in India. This triumphal arch was built by the Mughal Emperor Akbar in 1575 on the southern wall of the courtyard, after he defeated the King of Khandesh or Gujarat in 1573.

Description

The name Buland Darwaza means High Door and this victory arch has the height of 176 feet from ground level and 134 feet over the top step. Very striking even from quite a distance, Buland Darwaza is a magnificent structure built in red sandstone with ornamentation in white marble. The calligraphic inscriptions from the Quran on its front and pillars and chattris on its height make the arch an impressive sight. The Buland Darwaza is also indication of the religious tolerance of Akbar the Great, evident from the inscription upon it attributed to Jesus Christ - "The World is but a bridge, pass over but build no houses on it."

How to reach

To reach the Buland Darwaza in Agra, by air you have to land at the Agra airport, which is 7 km from the city center. From Delhi, it takes only 40 minutes to reach Agra by flight. The main railway station is Agra Cantonment. The main bus stands in Agra are Agra Fort and Idgah bus stand. There are many luxury taxis, coaches or buses that drive to Agra every day

Jama Masjid

Agra is well-known as being home to the wonderful Taj Mahal - one of the Seven Wonders of the World. The gracefully designed mausoleums, the fort and the palaces reminds of the Mughal architectural brilliance. Besides the Taj Mahal, other popular tourist spots in Agra are the Agra Fort, Itmad-Ud-Daulah's Tomb, Chini Ka Rauza, Rambagh Gardens, Fatehpur Sikri, etc. One such tourist attraction in Agra is the Jama Masjid, located right in the middle of the Fatehpur Sikri.

Background

Popularly known as the Jami Masjid, the Jama Masjid in Agra is perhaps the largest mosque in India. Overlooking Agra Fort railway station, the Jami Masjid or Friday Mosque was built by Shah Jahan in 1648 and dedicated to his favorite daughter, Jahanara Begum.

Description

Posted on a high podium approached by stairs, with five arched entrances to the courtyard, the mosque is crowned by three large sandstone domes notable by their winding bands of marble. Jama Masjid, flanked by the Zenana Rauza and the Jammat Khana hall on either side, is built in a manner that underlines its importance as a sacred place of worship.

Inlaid geometric designs, colored tiles and calligraphic inscriptions adorn the walls of the Jama Masjid. The massive central courtyard in the mosque has served as a haven for prayer and meditation for the devoted over the centuries. The tomb of the celebrated Sufi saint Sheikh Salim Chisti is located within the Jama Masjid complex.

Along the wings of the main prayer wall, large enough to accommodate 10,000 men at a time, panels of magnificently inlaid sandstone add a feminine touch. The building comprises of pillared Dalan, a beautiful Chhajja and the Chhatri on the roof. The main Iwan of the building is rather simple and contains a central arch with geometrical designs.

The entrance to the Jama Masjid Agra is approached through the massive gate Buland Darwaza, one of the highest gateways in the world, standing 40 meters high from ground level. It was constructed by Emperor Akbar to celebrate his victory in the Khandesh military campaign.

How to reach Jama Masjid

To reach the Jama Masjid in Agra, by air you have to land at the Agra airport, which is 7 km from the city center. From Delhi, it takes only 40 minutes to reach Agra by flight. The main railway station is Agra Cantonment. The main bus stands in Agra are Agra Fort and Idgah bus stand. There are many luxury taxis, coaches or buses that drive to Agra every day.

Tomb of Itimad Ud Daulah

Home to perhaps some of the finest examples of architecture in the world, Agra is a historian's paradise. Some of the treasures of architecture that grace the city include the Taj Mahal, Agra Fort and Itimad-ud-Daulah's Tomb. The Tomb of Itimad Ud Daulah was constructed by the Mughal queen Nur Jahan between 1622 and 1628 where her father Itimad Ud Daulah was buried. Itimad Ud Daulah or Mirza Ghiyas-ud-din or Ghiyas Beg was the father of Nur Jahan, the Mughal empress and wife of Jahangir. He was later also made a minister and a trusted treasurer in Akbar's court. It was as a tribute to him, that Nur Jahan built the mausoleum after his death.

Location

Located on the western bank of the Yamuna River, near the Yamuna Bridge Railway Station, the Tomb or mausoleum of Itimad-ud-Daulah is one of the best examples of the perfect blend of Mughal and local architecture. Well-connected to the other cities of the region, Agra can be easily reached from nearby cities like:

- Khajuraho
- Varanasi
- Delhi

Architecture

The tomb itself is one of the best examples of architecture of the region. Said to be one of the most important influences behind the architecture of the Taj Mahal, the Tomb of Itimad Ud Daulah is one of the finest examples of a specific genre of mausoleum architecture called a Tomb in a Garden. The construction is such that the tomb resembles a jewel-box set in the midst of a garden. Tranquil and lush green, the garden where the tomb is constructed is set on the banks of the river Yamuna. Famous for being the first tomb in the entirety of India to be built entirely of white marble, the Tomb of Itimad Ud Daulah is a must see for all visitors visiting the historic city of Agra. A perfect example of Islamic architecture, the tomb is characterized by arched entrances, octagonal shaped towers or minarets, use of exquisitely carved floral patterns, intricate marble-screen work and inlay work. However, added to this is the influence of the locality that manifests itself in the absence of a dome and the presence of a closed kiosk on top of this building as well as the use of chhatris (small domed canopies, supported by pillars) atop the four towers (minarets) instead of proper domes, which is more reflective of the Islamic style of architecture.

Taj Mahal Museum

Taj Mahal Museum in Agra is one of the most famous museums in Agra, which is visited by hundreds of tourists who wish to delve deep into the history of Taj. The Taj Museum is located within the complex of Taj Mahal. It is located to the left of the platform near the chief gate of the Taj Mahal. The Taj Museum of Agra provides the opportunity to the tourists and visitors to take a close look at the original pieces of drawings of this magnificent marble monument. The study of the drawings indicates the level of accuracy and precision that had been initiated in planning the structure of the Taj Mahal. No wonder that the Taj still features among the Seven Wonders of the World.

The Taj Museum remains open from 10 o' clock in the morning to 5 o' clock in the afternoon. These drawings also show the layout of the graves. Drawings of the interiors show the position of the graves in such precision that the foot of the graves faces the spectator from any angle. Besides, there are many other bewitching collections that will catch the fancy of the tourists.

History of Taj Mahal Museum, Agra

Agra Taj Mahal Museum lies within the complex of Taj Mahal- one of the greatest symbols of the eternal love. The museum was constructed in 1982 and it is to be found in the Jal Mahal, a Mahal inside the Taj Mahal.

Description of Taj Mahal Museum, Agra

The Taj Mahal Museum in Agra houses royal ornaments, amazing paintings, portraits of Mughal emperors and many more interesting items. The Taj Museum remains closed on Fridays.

It is a big museum comprising of two floors and has three galleries along with a chief hall. The Taj Mahal Museum, as the name suggests, displays all those things in connection to the creation of Taj Mahal. There are a total of one hundred and twenty one antiques showcased in the Agra Taj Mahal museum. These things can be broadly classified into Mughal manuscripts, Mughal miniature paintings, inscription samples, royal decrees, drawings and plans of Taj Mahal. Some more exquisite items are also exhibited in the museum like arms, utensils, specimen of decorative pieces, marble pillars, etc.

The main hall showcases the most significant items. Tourists can take a look at the portraits of Shah Jahan and Mumtaz Mahal, his beloved wife. These are seen in an ornate wooden frame. Imitations of coins, which were minted in Agra, are also on display. Like the Taj Mahal, the museum which stands within it, is also a wonder and an attractive place to be visited by all tourists across the world. Nominal fees are charged at the entrance of the gate. Everyday, millions of people come to visit Taj Mahal- one of the Seven Wonders of the World. It is quite obvious that the museum which displays antiques related to Taj Mahal will also be visited by the curious travelers.

Akbar's Tomb at Sikandra
One of the most important bases of Mughal power, Agra is home to some of the finest examples of Mughal architecture. One of these is Akbar's Tomb at Sikandra , where one of the greatest

emperors in the world lies buried. Perhaps the greatest monarch India has ever seen and definitely the most powerful and able ruler of the Mughal dynasty, Akb ar supervised the construction of the tomb himself during his lifetime. The rest of the tomb was completed by his son Jahangir after Akbar's death.

Location

Located at a distance of just 4 kilometers away from Agra, Sikandra is named after Sikander Lodhi.

Architecture

A perfect blend of Hindu, Christian, Islamic, Buddhist, Jain styles of architectures, Akbar's Tomb is just like the ideals of the great monarch himself an amalgamation of the positivities of different cultures. The most important aspect of the construction is that it shows the developing style of Mughal architecture. The tomb comprises of three-storey minarets on four corners which is perhaps the most characteristic feature of Islamic architecture. Another important feature of early Mughal architecture is also evident in its construction which is the combination of red sandstone and marble, a feature that was to be replaced completely by marble in the later period.

A five storey building the tomb also houses the remains of Akbar's daughters, Shakrul Nisha Begum and Aram Bano.

Moti Masjid

There are many notable holy places in Agra of which Moti Masjid in Agra occupies special position of distinction. It is held that one who has visited the St. Basils Cathedral in Moscow will feel that it contains close structural resemblance with that. Sitting in the compound of the Agra Fort where river Yamuna is also present in the backdrop, this mosque is very frequently visited by the travelers. Its shiny domes are built with light white marble which lends it a very velvety look and adds a sparkle to its beauty.

History of Moti Masjid, Agra

The Agra Moti Masjid was built by the very powerful emperor and a connoisseur of art famously called Shah Jahan. During the rule of Shah Jahan the Mughal emperor, numerous architectural wonders were built. Today most of these are the feast for the eyes. However coming back to the Moti Masjid it can be said that Moti Masjid earned the epithet Pearl Mosque for it shined like a pearl. It is held that this mosque was constructed by Shah Jahan for his members of royal court.

Description of Moti Masjid, Agra

Moti Masjid in Agra is a delightful sight for eyes. Its architectural features are quite similar to that of the St. Basils Cathedral in Moscow. It is located in the vicinity of River Yamuna and enjoys its position in the compound of the invincible Agra Fort. It contains three domes built of light white marble. The three marble domes stand on the red sandstone walls. Looking at its structure you will come across the splendid symmetrical design of the mosque. Sitting to the right of the hall Diwan-E-Aam of the Agra Fort, the mosque mesmerizes travelers with its velvety appearance.

The Agra Moti Masjid is very close to the city center. Hence reaching this place is never a problem. To reach here you can avail the apt bus services from the Power House Bus Stand. The railway station is also very near to it. This apart, the Agra Airport is situated to the south-west of Agra Fort. To come here directly form the airport you need to cover a distance of 8 km.

Taj Mahal Garden
Taj Mahal is the most important monument in Agra which is the symbol of eternal love. It features among the Seven Wonders of the World. Taj Mahal incorporates both Persian and Hindu elements; therefore Taj Mahal flaunts a Persian style garden.

Garden in Persian culture is a very important motif as Quran equates a gorgeous garden with ecstasy. Stretched from the main gateway to the doorway of this mausoleum, the lush green Taj Mahal garden in Agra is based on symmetry and geometrical measurements.

Description of Taj Mahal Garden, Agra

Taj Mahal gardens, Agra mostly feature religious motifs. The Water Garden, for example, is divided into four equal squares by two marble canals. The garden is bounded by cypress trees and fountains; the garden conjures up the Islamic concept of heaven where rivers of water, milk, wine and honey flow. At the center of the garden and the mausoleum a lotus shaped tank is located. The water in the tank acts as a reflective facade and the image of Taj can be seen on the water from any spot in the garden. The exclusive location of the tank helps the mirror like viewing of this extravagant monument of love.

The Taj Mahal Garden in Agra features a Persian style garden which symbolizes heaven, since Quran describes paradise as a beautiful garden. On the other hand the water garden of the Agra Taj Mahal garden feature two marble canals with fountains and lined with cypress trees (symbolizing death).

This divides the garden into four identical squares (Islam recognizes four to be a holy number), the stone paved pathways again subdivides each flower bed into 4, making total of 16 flower beds.

The tank has been arranged to provide a crystal clear view of Taj in its water. The view looks wonderful with the reflection of Taj amidst the green cypress trees.

Taj Mahal Garden in Agra displays a unique irrigation system. Water in the canals was drawn from the river using purs, a system of drawing water physically from river using bucket and ropes. For irrigation the water from the overflowing canals was used. The north-south canals had its water bay through fountains and east-west canal had its water bay through a intermingling with north-south canal. It has been made very uniquely which still astonishes the tourists who come here to view the eternal monument of love.

Shah Jahan Park

A hop to Agra is not only an exciting experience of life but its very enriching and pleasant experience too to cherish for entire life. Here you will come across the most enduring symbols of love, the Taj Mahal which also enjoys a place of pride among the

Seven Wonders of the World. The beauty of the Agra Fort can not also be missed. However if these are the places to bask in the architectural glory of the bygone days and learn about their historical connections then there are several gardens in Agra to simply seek some relaxed and pleasurable moments of life. And one such garden that stands out from the rest because of its picturesque beauty and enchanting ambience is Shah Jahan Park in Agra.

Agra Shah Jahan Park is a beautiful Mughal garden with lush green expanse. It stretches towards Taj Mahal on west direction.

History of Shah Jahan Park, Agra

The Shah Jahan Park in Agra was laid out during the rule of Mughal Empire. This park is named after the very powerful and famous emperor of Mughal period called Shah Jahan. It was during his rule that magnificent and splendid architectures were created among which the majestic Taj Mahal, built in the memory of his beloved wife Mumtaz Mahal, warrant a special mention. He was deposed from the throne by his son Aurangzeb in 1658 and detained in the Agra fort.

Description of Shah Jahan Park, Agra

Agra Shah Jahan Park is counted among the very attractive Mughal gardens in India. Its lush green expanse and emerald colored floors create an indelible impression on the minds of the onlookers who visit this site to enjoy a great time. The beautifully laid out green stretch of the garden is an ideal place to relax and catch fresh breath. This park offers an enjoyable break to indulge in leisurely stroll on way to Taj Mahal. It is very adjacent to Motilal Nehru Park too that again offers easy access to Taj Mahal. Besides there is an extensive Golf Course which is a very popular destination for the tourists.

The Shah Jahan Park in Agra is a perfect place for those who want to get engrossed in the pristine air of Agra and are intrigued by the rich history of the town. This garden is mostly visited early in the morning or little late in the evening by joggers and pleasure seekers.

Spiritual Museum

The Museums in Agra rank among the popular Agra Tourist Attractions. Agra is one of the most visited tourist destinations in India and is famous for its rich tradition and heritage. The forts, tombs and historical buildings and ancient specimens have led to the growth of a variety of museums in Agra. The Spiritual

Museum, Agra is one such museum which exhibits the well known cultural and historical specimens and relics of the Mughal period.

The Spiritual Museum in Agra is one of the recent museums in Agra. By visiting the Spiritual Museum, tourists get a feel of the ancient history, tradition and culture of the city. They can observe and study plenty of artifacts, historical relics and ancient specimens in the museum.

The location of the Spiritual Museum Agra also makes it very popular. The museum is located within few kilometers from the spectacular Taj Mahal. Travelers who visit the Taj Mahal can come to the museum on the way. The museum is spread over a beautiful field which is surrounded by gardens and fountains. The gate of the museum is beautifully designed with a blend of traditional and modern touch. The front of the museum is designed like a shikara, which is wonderfully decorated. The museum remains open all over the week and draws hundreds of tourists.

The Spiritual Museum Agra has been established by a new formed movement, which is known as the 'Brahma Kumaris'. The followers of this movement believe in the concept of the self realization of God. The interior of the museum is also beautifully decorated with a plethora of colors and designs. Various chambers of the museum provide a deep insight into the various religious beliefs and cultures in the country. At times, yoga and meditation workshops are also held here.

One can easily reach the Spiritual Museum in Agra. The museum is easily accessible from the main city center by various modes of transportation. Regular bus, car and auto services are available. Plenty of tours are also undertaken to the Spiritual museum. There are half day tours and are offered by the travel agencies and the local tourist board.

Ram Bagh

The Mughal emperors were perhaps one of the greatest rulers of the country and leading influences in shaping the country into what she is today. Much of the influences of the dynasty can still be seen all around the country today, notable amongst which is the dynasty's architectural prowess. The Mughals were responsible for the construction of a number of forts, palaces, tombs and gardens. The Mughal gardens of pleasure were especially noteworthy. In these gardens of pleasure, the Mughal rulers tried to reincarnate the image of paradise as conceptualized by most Islamic texts. One of these gardens is the Rambagh Gardens in Agra.

Location

Conceptualized by Babur, the first of the Mughal emperors in India, the Rambagh Garden is located in Agra, Uttar Pradesh just 3 kms away from the Tomb of Itimad Ud Daulah and 500 meters away from the Chini ka Rauza.

Foundation

The Rambagh Gardens or Bagh-i-gul Afshan as they are also known were established by Babur and later renovated by Nur Jahan, wife of Jahangir and one of the most influential Mughal empresses.

Architecture

The Garden which is also known as Bagh-i-Gul Afshan is planned following the Charbagh pattern which consists of four main divisions crisscrossed by paths and waterways. Water which forms a very integral part of Islam is almost likened to life in these pleasure parks. The main source of water in the Rambagh Gardens is the Yamuna from which water is distributed all around the park in a series of three cascades developed over three terraces. Besides these there are stairs on either side of the water channels, fountains, an island platform and two pavilions on either side of the main water channel, that truly go a long way into converting the Rambagh Gardens into a real paradise.

Mehtab Bagh

The Mehtab Bagh in Agra is laid out in just right symmetry and alignment with the Taj Mahal and it was intentionally built as an integral part of the original design of the Taj Mahal during the period from 1631 to 1635 A.D. It has been named as the 'Mehtab Bagh' or 'The Moon Garden' because it is an ideal point for viewing the Taj Mahal in romantic moonlight.

History of Mehtab Bagh, Agra

When the world famous Taj Mahal was being constructed 350 years ago a moonlight garden named Mehtab Bagh was laid just across the Yamuna River. It was laid alongside the northern waterfront. The place was once an oasis with sweet-smelling flowers, shaded pavilions, fountain jets and reflecting pools but it ceased to exist in the due course of history. Gradually the site became barren and lost its earlier charm. Once you visit the Mehtab Bagh in Agra you will get transformed into the glorious Mughal era. This is one of the most famous gardens in Agra.

Description of Mehtab Bagh, Agra

Agra Mehtab Bagh is a 25-acre plot has now transformed into an epicenter for the top court-ordered project to set up protective greenways around the Taj. As the land is reclaimed, historians and geographers from around the world are trying to learn about the wonderful garden that once existed near this oasis. An advance technology inspired from Iran has been applied to bloom the Mehtab Bagh once again. Mehtab Bagh in Agra will again flower with fragrant and colorful flowers which will surely produce the sweet smell of the glorious past.

The growing attention to Agra Mehtab Bagh can be credited to the escalating concern for the Taj and its grounds, which are in danger by urban sprawl, too many tourists, and air pollution that eats away into the shrine's marble exterior. The lush gardens that once lined the riverbanks on either side of the Taj may flourish again in a scheme to protect it from further damages. Conservationists uphold that a buffer zone of greenery would keep development at bay and help remedy local air, noise, and water pollution. Much of the land for the greenbelt had already been acquired through a previous proposal to establish a 340-acre national park around the Taj. While yours to Agra a visit to this opulent garden will mark you treat your eyes far away from the hustle bustle of the busy town.

Mangleshwar Temple

Agra abounds in numerous religious places. The special feature of the holy places in Agra is that these are established to cater to every religion and sect. For Muslim community it has mosques, for Sikhs it features gurudwaras, for Hindus it boasts of some of the most revered temples. In some or the other way the religious places in Agra enjoy historical significance. But at the same time there are some which can supposedly be found without such association. One of these kinds of temples is Mangleshwar Temple in Agra.

The Agra Mangleshwar Temple is a very noted tourist attractions. Like other holy places, this temple also enjoys religious and architectural significance. Every year a surge of thousands of devotees can be noticed. It is located towards west of the Agra city center in Gokal Pura region. Its popularity is huge in the suburbs of the city and native people. The best time to visit this temple is festive season.

Description of Mangleshwar Temple, Agra

The Mangleshwar Temple in Agra is reckoned among the most celebrated religious sites of Agra. It is situated towards the western part of the Agra city center in the Gokal Pura area. This temple is very lavishly bedecked during festivities and exemplifies the religious diversity in Agra. Truly speaking, a visit during Hindu festivities will bring in spotlight the Hindu style of worship. The entire ambience of the temple acquires a gorgeous, animated and colorful look.

If you are also interested in paying Agra Mangleshwar Temple a visit and basking in its architectural splendor and religious importance then do come here. It is very near to the central railway line. This rail line connects the northern and southern regions of the Agra city. You can also come here by Ramratan Road.

From the Mangleshwar Temple in Agra you can head for other attractive spots of tourist interest that comprise of both historical sites and religious places. You will truly enjoy the diversion here by visiting diverse types of attractions.

Dayalbagh Gardens
Agra is one of the most important cities of India from the point of view of tourism. The city has a number of varied attractions

that are guaranteed to please people of varied tastes. Thus, where history is represented by places like the Taj Mahal, Agra Fort and Fatehpur Sikri, sceneries and the beauty of nature is celebrated by the presence of gardens like the Rambagh Gardens and the Dayalbagh Gardens.

Location

Located at a distance of just around 15 Km from Agra, the Dayalbagh Gardens form a major tourist attraction of the area and are generally included in most tours conducted in the vicinity of Agra.

Foundation

The Dayalbagh Gardens have been founded in the memory of Shiv Dayal Sahib the founder of the Radhasoami Satsang Movement, a religious movement that was begun in 1861. The movement basically follows a code that is an amalgamation of a number of other religions such as Hinduism, Christianity, Sikhism and Buddhism.

Architecture

The architecture of the Dayalbagh Gardens follows much of the same pattern of amalgamation of the traits of different religions like the Radhasoami Satsang movement itself. Thus, this beautiful memorial gives examples of different architectural styles such as those that can be found in temples, gurudwaras, viharas and mosques all across the country. Impressive at a height of around 110 feet, the memorial is built completely in white marble with majestic pillars.

An interesting feature of the memorial is that the construction work at the site is a continuous process. This is due to a belief of the followers of the faith which insists that tending the memorial should be a constant process.

Chini ka Rauza

Agra can definitely be termed as the hub of historical tourism in India. Almost each and every nook and corner of this ancient city relates a tale of its own, sharing secrets which time had thought to be buried within the silent bricks of Agra. Of the many historical attractions of the city, one of the lesser-known ones is the Chini ka Rauza , the tomb of Allama Afzal Khan Mullah of Shiraz, built in 1635.

Location

Located at a distance of just around 1 Km from Itimad ud Daulah's Tomb, Chini ka Rauza is the tomb of Allama Afzal Khan Mullah of Shiraz, a scholar and poet who was the Prime Minister of the Mughal Emperor Shah Jahan. A notable feature amongst the many attractions that Agra offers, Chini ka Rauza is the only example of Persian architecture in the city.

Architecture

The structural design of the Chini ka Rauza is like the rest of the architectural masterpieces constructed by the Mughals a work of excellence. Built during the reign of Shah Jahan, at a time when the architectural prowess of the Mughals was at its peak, Chini ka Rauza is a must see for tourists to Agra. The most distinctive feature of the tomb is the colorful tiles or chini, from which the mausoleum gets its name. Rectangular in shape, the tomb is constructed mainly of brown stone, which today is sadly falling prey to negligence and crumbling away. The walls of the tomb are adorned with inscriptions and colored tiles that give a distinctive look to the structure.

However, perhaps the most significant feature of the tomb is the Afghan-style rounded dome that is adorned with inscriptions from Islamic texts.

The Tomb

The central chamber which actually houses the tomb is an octagonal chamber that consists of eight arched corners. This chamber is connected to the side halls and outer porches through four square chambers. The central arch, which is one of the most prominent architectural features of the tomb, is adorned with inscriptions marked with blue colored tiles.

Bageshwarnath Temple

There are a good number of holy places in Agra, among which Bageshwarnath Temple in Agra enjoys a special significance. Situated in the posh locale off the Ramratan Road in the northern region of Agra, the temple is not more than two kilometres away from the heart of the city. The temple is well-connected by a good network of roads and is easily accessible. St. John's College and the Sales Tax Office are situated very near to this temple. Bageshwarnath Temple in Agra is very popular in the neighborhood of Raja ki Mundi.

Description of Bageshwarnath Temple, Agra

Agra's Bageshwarnath Temple is venerated by both the locals and the foreign tourists. The temple registers the footfall of a large number of devotees all round the year. The temple, apart from being significant from the religious point of view, also acts as a distinguishing landmark of the place. During the Hindu festivals, Bageshwarnath Temple, Agra takes on a festive spirit.

The temple is illuminated and looks gorgeous. The bright and colorful adornments lend a unique charm to the temple. The temple complex becomes the center of all festivities.

If you are out on a religious tour in Agra, then there are a number of places of the religious importance that you can pay a visit to en route to Bageshwarnath Temple, Agra. Among these popular temples the Shri Krishna Pranami Temple and the Arya Samaj Temple warrant a special visit. If you have some time to spare you could also make a short trip to the memorial of Swami Maharaj in Dayal Bagh. This is a highly venerated of the religious places that are visited by thousands of devotees every year.

Guru Ka Taal
There are several architectural splendors in Agra to relish. Each possesses a distinct quality and flavor. The interesting part however is that most of the sites undeniably have historical and architectural importance but along with that there are some sites that share cultural and religious significance too. The example of the holy places in Agra can very conveniently be brought here. As the point of discussion is that some Agra attractions enjoy historical, architectural and religious significance so the mention of Guru Ka Taal in Agra becomes a must.

The Agra Guru Ka Taal is the most revered and venerated place of the Sikhs dwelling in Agra. Of the 10 Sikh prophets four are supposed to have visited this holy place. This beautiful gurudwara is located within the boundaries of Sikandra and every year it witnesses huge tourist influx.

History of Guru Ka Taal, Agra

Guru Ka Taal in Agra was erected in 1970s. Its construction was completed with the contributions and laborious efforts of Sant Sadhu Singh Mauni. A peep into the historical records will reveal that it was established at the site where Guru Tegh Bahadur surrendered to to Aurangazeb, the Mughal King. This apart, it is also said that Tal was a reservoir. It was decorated with intricate stone carvings.

Description of Guru Ka Taal, Agra

The Agra Guru Ka Taal is a holy place of worship for the Sikh. The four Sikh gurus of the 10 Sikh gurus are said to have paid it a visit. Enjoying both historical and religious importance, this gurudwara attracts end number of devotees and tourists. Every year thousands of devotees gather here to pay homage to the great Sikh guru. This 17th century red stone structure is reckoned among the magnificent architectural wonders of India.

Boasting elaborate stone carvings and 8 towers of the 12 original towers, this gurudwara beckons travelers from far and away to bask in its glory.

The Guru Ka Taal in Agra is a very popular tourist attraction. It is kept open from dawn to dusk everyday. You don't need to pay admission charges to enter its premises. To reach this gurudwara you need to come to Baluchpura Railway Station which is just 5 km away from Sikandra.

Caleb Gray

Best Time to Visit Agra

Agra is a major tourist destination owing to the UNESCO World Heritage sites and the main one being the Taj Mahal. The tourists flock into the city throughout the year to experience the reflection of the Mughal era, it is never a bad time to visit Agra and witness the authenticity. However, visiting during the cooler months of October to March is pleasurable and better. Agra experiences extreme temperatures in summers and winters, the best time recommended visiting is in the months with moderate climate.

Where to Visit in Agra & When

Agra during Summer- From March till June

Summers in Agra are hot and dry; sometimes the temperature soars up to 45 degree Celsius. The night times are relatively cooler. This is not an ideal time to visit the city but not impossible. The benefit of traveling around summers is that the crowd is less and hotel deals are better. Carry some light cotton wears and sunscreens and enjoy the trip.

Agra during Monsoon- From July till September

The monsoon occasional but it generally begin from July and come as a relief from the hot summers by the locals. The showers are heavy, dropping the temperature in between 25 to 35 degrees Celsius. The view of the drenched Taj Mahal is spectacular and rare. Agra being a semi arid region receives the annual average rainfall of about 400 mm.

Agra during Winter- From November till March

Experience cool and pleasant climate during the winter season, the temperature can come down to 2 degree Celsius in the peak month. Winter is characterized by thick fogs, however, it is an ideal time for the tourists to explore and walk around the city at leisure. The temperature ranges from 8 to 14 degree Celsius.

he fairs and festivals are mostly celebrated during the winter seasons, Taj Mahotsav (February); Ram Bharat, Kailash Fair and Bateshwar Fair are the major attractions meant for your visit.

How to Reach in Agra

Agra is famous not only in India but also all over the world for the beautiful monument as well as a symbol of love. Agra attracts a lot of tourists every year and leaves them completely mesmerized. Often the tourists, basically the international are confronted with the problem of how to reach Agra! But Agra being a chief city of Uttar Pradesh is well connected by flights, trains and road transport.

By Air

Reaching Agra by flight is the most convenient mode of transport as Agra airport has all the major domestic flights landing in. Both government as well as private airways flies to and from Agra. The shortest flight to Agra is the one from Delhi that takes around 40 minutes to reach. The airport of Agra is located at a distance of 7 km from the city center.

By Rail

There is no hassle as how to reach Agra since the city of Agra is well connected by rail networks and a lot of trains connect Delhi and Agra, which also include the luxury trains like the Palace on Wheels. Agra Station is also popular as Agra Cantonment Station.

By Road

Travel to Agra is even more interesting by the road transport as Agra has excellent road networks which is the national highway connecting Delhi and Agra. The luxury coaches and bus services help reaching Agra quite conveniently and the journey takes about four hours. The tourists especially can witness the landscape and the rural life even more closely when they will travel by the rail or the road networks and it will simply enrich their travel experience.

The major bus stands of Agra are Idgah bus stand and Agra Fort bus stand.

Monuments in Agra

The city of Agra is mostly visited for the beautiful Taj Mahal, but there are many more grand monuments worth seeing when you travel to this historic city. Agra was ruled by Mughal dynasty for a long period of time and under its reign Agra has been endowed with many fine buildings and monuments. Monuments in Agra will leave you awestruck and mesmerized. Great monuments of Agra include the Agra Fort, which embraces grand halls and palaces and the tomb of Itimad-ud-Daulah, a model for the Taj Mahal. Agra is one of the richest heritage sites in India where many remarkable Mughal monuments can be found. Monuments in Agra India are diversified from the splendid Taj Mahal to sober tombs like Akbar's mausoleum at Sikandra. The monuments in Agra have exceptional architectural features and are the epitome of the best examples of Mughal architecture in India.

Mughal monuments in Agra will fascinate you and make you walk down the corridors of the glorious past. The marvelous feats of engineering are behind the creations of the massive structures such as the Buland Darwaza and the Jami Masjid in Fatehpur Sikri and the spectacular Taj Mahal in Agra, are awe inspiring.

Agra Monuments continue to astonish architects and engineers in recent times when technology and the work system have advanced in a tremendous way. The architects of that time were deprived of latest advances still there were masters at their field which resulted in creating such monuments. Engineers of today are left spell bound with the astounding ingenious systems of water supply and natural cooling of earliest monuments of Agra. Artists and historians value the fine inlay work, the decorative devices and the synthesis of Indian and Persian elements seen in these monuments of the Indo-Saracenic school of Architecture, which boomed under the Mughal Empire. The monuments in Agra India are an enduring piece of India's architectural heritage.

The Agra Fort is positioned on a bank of the River Yamuna in Agra. This massive monument in Agra has many palaces, gardens mosques within its complex.

At a distance of four kilometers from the city of Agra is the mausoleum of the Mughal emperor Akbar. This famous monument in Agra has a wonderful culmination of Hindu, Christian, Islamic, Buddhist, Jain motifs.

Another great monument of Agra is the Chini-Ka-Rauza which is a tomb of glazed tiles and is a monument in honor of the poet-scholar and later the Prime Minister of Shah Jahan, Allama Afzel Khal Mullah Shukrullah of Shiraz.

Taj Mahal, the mausoleum of Mughal Emperor Shah Jana's chief wife, Mumtaz Mahal, has become synonymous with India. This is one of the splendid monuments in Agra. It's curving, gently swelling dome and the square base upon which its rests so lightly is a recognizable image on hundreds of brochures and travel books. The Taj is unquestionably one of the most impressive buildings of the world. It is reckoned among man's most prized creations and is invariably included in the list of the world's foremost wonders and is legendary for its architectural magnificence and a esthatic beauty.

Agra Excursions

On Tours to Uttar Pradesh the most fascinating travel destination you will find is Agra. Every tourist on an escapade to measure the splendor of the attractive spots in Uttar Pradesh makes a point to visit Agra that houses one of the very elegant Seven Wonders of the World like Taj Mahal. However along with Taj Mahal, the tourists also engage in exploring the charming influence of the imposing Agra Fort, the very gorgeous Rambagh Gardens, Itimad Ud Daulah and the Chini ka Rauza. There are innumerable sights to relish. But once all the sites are covered the pleasure travelers like to take excursions from Agra to nearby destinations.

On Agra excursions the travelers basically head for mostly two destinations. They like to visit Fatehpur Sikri, the ruined fortified city. It usually takes a daylong travel to reach here. But for the convenience an overnight stay is suggested in the hotels in Fatehpur Sikri. Fatehpur Sikri having served as a capital for Akbar, the powerful Mughal emperor, was soon abandoned after it suffered water scarcity.

Today this city is taken in to enjoy strolls within the ruined city walls. This apart, on excursions around Agra this place is best to relish the splendid charm of mosques, palaces and tombs. Some of the must visit attractions include Jama Masjid, Buland

Darwaza, Tomb of Sheikh Salim Chisti, Palace of Jodh Bai, Hawa Mahal, Panch Mahal, Birbal Bhavan, Diwan-I-Khas, Diwan-I-Am, Hiran Minar and Karawan Sarai.

Other most sought after destination on excursions from Agra is Mathura, the birthplace of the Hindu deity Lord Krishna. It is a very popular pilgrimage site for Hindus. Some of the fascinating spots that constitute the impeccable beauty of this city are Dwarkadheesh Temple, Potara-Kund, Katra Masjid, Kans Qila, Sati Burj and Vishram Ghat.

Gardens in Agra

Agra features as not only one of the popular tourist destinations in India but also in the world. Millions of tourists from across the globe come to Agra and visit the numerous tourist spots in and around the city. Apart from the magnificent Gardens, buildings and museums, the Gardens in Agra are also the eternal favorite with the travelers.

Agra is the home to many spectacular parks and gardens. Some of the most famous Agra gardens are the Mehtab Bagh, Shah Jahan Park, Dayal Bagh Gardens, Ram Bagh, Aalsi Bagh, Taj Mahal Garden and the Mughal Gardens. The Taj Mahal Garden is a long stretch of verdant greenery, which can be seen from the main gateway of the Taj Mahal and stretches to the entrance of the burial chambers. The Aalsi Bagh has an appealing romantic connection with its name.

It is believed that the famous Mughal Emperor Akbar spent six days in the garden lying idle or Aalsi to convince his darling to agree to his proposal. The Mughal Gardens in the Agra Fort is another glorious garden. The meaning of Mehtab Bagh is the Moon Lit Garden and the striking reflection of Taj Mahal in its pool is a lovely sight in a full moon night. The Ram Bagh is one of the oldest of the many Mughal gardens of Agra. Some feel the Taj is best viewed on a full moon night, others find it ethereal at dawn while some insist that it is sensuous at sunset. It was built by Babur, the founder of the great Mughal dynasty. Jehangir's wife Nur Jahan made further additions to enhance the exquisiteness of the garden. The Shahjahan Garden is no less striking than the other gardens.

Dayal Bagh Garden, also known as the "garden of the Supreme Lord", is regarded as one of the important Agra gardens. The Dayalbagh Gardens would surely be an appealing place to visit for connoisseurs of art, who would love to appreciate the skilled artisans and marble cutters at work.

One of the famous gardens in Agra is the The Shah Jahan Garden acclaimed to be the most beautiful Mughal garden in India. This is an astonishingly decorated area with a lush green spread. The emerald colored floors of the Shah Jahan Park expands towards the west of the Taj Mahal.

Shopping in Agra

Besides making its mark as a most sought-after tourist destination, Agra is also a heaven for the shopaholics who can't overcome the temptation of splurging on shopping. Once you are through with your sightseeing activities, shopping in Agra is the most favorable alternative. Apart from the various architectural splendors that dot the city, Agra is also equally renowned for its exquisite handicrafts and other art works. So if you have a thing for anything aesthetic or just want to add to your collection of beautifully hand crafted items, then shopping in the Agra is the ideal way to satiate your shopping urge.

Often touted as the shopper's paradise, Agra is a juxtaposition of quaint, bustling markets and contemporary shopping malls.

During the Mughal rule, when the lavish Mughal courts were held in Agra, the markets in Agra were frequented by the skilled craftsmen who brought with them their best wares in the hope to get the patronage of the Emperor. Even during those times, people used to experience an inexplicable high while shopping in Agra. The historical documents corroborate the fact that Empress Noor Jahan took a keen interest in opulent and exquisite embroidery and textiles, so much so that she employed a number of female dress makers who were engaged in the task of stitching out impressive and grand robes both for the Emperors as well as the courtiers.

One remarkable fact about Agra shopping is that the items that were once exclusively meant for the royalty are now made available to the discerning customers.

Agra is replete with a number of shops where you can get a number of items that you won't find anywhere else in the world. Agra has gained international repute for its fine marble and leatherwork. You can't resist the temptation shop for some of the good quality leather products that include shoes, bags, belts and more. Shop in Agra for sandal and rose wood items that are found in the craft emporiums and that make for wonderful keepsakes. The rugs and carpets will also captivate your attention. Woven by master craftsmen, these products are inimitable in their quality and the skilled craftsmanship that they exemplify. When you are in Agra, you can't possibly miss out on the scrumptious Mughlai cuisine. The sweets petha and Gazak and the snack called dalmoth warrant special mention.

Bazaars in Agra
Some of the most popular shopping destinations in Agra comprise of the Sadar Bazaar, Kinari Bazaar and the Munro Road. The U.P State Emporium called Gangotri should also not be given a miss while shopping in Agra. If you wish to browse through a good collection of handicrafts, the Shilpagram Crafts Fair is the place you should head to. For souvenirs and keepsakes, the U.P Handlooms and UPICA at Sanjay Place on M.G Road are the best places.

Bazaars in Agra
On Agra Tour, you are not caught with shopping fever, it is not possible. Apart from relishing the beauty and grandeur of the historical and architectural sites of Agra, shopping becomes a must-task for you. You should not skip this opportunity. While traveling in the city you will chance upon an array of bazaars in

Agra. The very sight of these bazaars will be so fascinating and engrossing that you will forget about the rest of the things and immediately head for the colorful markets to make your purchase.

Some of the very famous and must visit Agra bazaar areas are the Loha Mandi, Civil Line, Tajganj, Dayal Bagh and the Rakab Ganj area. Besides, shopping in Agra becomes a little bit of extra fun when you venture upon the areas like Taj Mahal Complex, Sardar Bazaar, Raja ki Mandi, Kinari Bazaar and the Sanjay Place.

While exploring the most vibrant and colorful bazaars in Agra you should not miss out on the souvenir shops. These shops are approved and recognized by the U.P Tourism and the Government Emporium. The advantage of visiting souvenir shops in Agra is that you can carry the memory of the pleasurable moments that you have spent here during vacations.

Along with buying souvenirs, you can also find stunning and striking items in the markets in Agra to adorn yourself and butter up your family and friends a bit. You can buy attractive chappals, bags, purses, decorative items, wall hangers and other leather products. It will be a true delight for your soul to shop handicraft items made of rose wood and sandalwood, brass and stone made show-pieces and colorful clothes and garments.

In the bazaars in Agra you will also get a good collection of books, electronic good and latest gadgets. For these items several book stores and shops that deal in electronic equipments are best to visit. This apart in case of medical urgency you can head for any of the several chemist shops located in the areas like Civil Line, Loha Mandi, Mantola, Rakabganj, Tajganj and others.

Fairs and Festivals in Agra

Agra is a beautiful city, which is visited by a crazy number of travelers from all around. Fair and festivals in Agra are quite colorful. If you visit the Mughal City during the celebrations, it is an ideal time to get a sneak-peak into the culture and traditions of the region. Following are some of the most popular fairs and festivals in Agra:

Taj Mahotsav

One of the most famous festivals in Agra, Taj Mahotsav is an annual event, which is organized in the month of February for 10 days. Close to the Taj Mahal, the Crafts Village or Shilpgram is the venue of the festival. The festival is organized by Uttar Pradesh Tourism to promote the art and craft of the region, made painstakingly by local craftsmen. The festival is a display of art, crafts, culture, traditional variety of food, and folk performances. Ghazal and Mushairas (poetry) performances is the other highlight. For children, there are camel and elephant rides.

The festival welcomes the spring season with zeal. The Mahotsav starts with a grand procession that has decorated camels and elephants, folk artists, accompanied by drumbeaters. Some of the best attractions at Taj Mahotsav include Chikankari from Lucknow, handmade carpets from Badohi, wood carvings from Saharanpur, silk from Varanasi, blue pottery from Khurja, Sapera dance from Rajasthan, Nautanki from Uttar Pradesh, Lavani from Maharashtra, and so on.

Bateshwar Fair

The town of Bateshwar is located at a distance of just 70 km from Agra. It is named after the presiding deity, Bateshwar Mahadeo. This town is known for its cultural as well as spiritual significance as it has 108 temples of several Hindu gods and goddess. An annual fair is organized here in the months of

October/November, dedicated to Lord Shiva. During this month-long event, thousands of devotees of the Lord take a dip in the holy waters of River Yamuna. Livestock and Cattle Fair is a part of this fair. The festivities can be seen in Agra too.

Ram Barat

Organized before Dussehra, Ram Barat is the special marriage procession of Lord Ram, which is organized every year in Agra. It is a part of Ramleela, which ends on the day of Dussehra, when Lord kills Ravana. At a special venue the palace of the Goddess Sita, Raja Janak, 'Janakpuri' is set-up. One of the highlights is the bedecked 'jhankis'. This venue becomes the base for the fair, which is visited by thousands of devotees of the Lord who come to witness the royal wedding.

The procession of Ram Barat commences from Lala Channomalji Ki Baradari, traversing through the lanes of the city, to arrive at Janakpuri venue. The idol of Lord Rama, along with his brothers on elephants, is kept on special chariot decorated with silver leaves. Their bejeweled headgears look fabulous. The role of female characters are played by the local teenaged boys.

Kailash Fair

Organized at a location, just 12 km away from Agra, Kailash Fair is held at Kailash temple for paying homage to Lord Shiva. The festival is organized in the month of August/September for celebrating the appearance of Lord Shiva as a stone lingam. Devotees from nearby places attend this fair.

Delhi

Situated on the banks of the Yamuna River, Agra is known for its rich culture and Mughal heritage. It was the Mughal capital from 1526 to 1658 and the emperors built majestic forts and monuments during their reign here. Taj Mahal, the undying symbol of love, makes Agra an unrivaled tourist destination. This marvel is at the zenith of Mughal architectural splendor. Agra tourist attractions are the reason why the domestic and international travelers throng this city throughout the year.

History of New Delhi

History of Delhi is an integral part of Delhi General Info. The capital city of India, Delhi bears the legacy of a glorious history. A city dotted with many places of interest and various forms of entertainment, Delhi has a charm of its own. The most popular tourist attractions of Delhi are the Red Fort, Jama Masjid, Chandni Chowk, Humayun's Tomb, India Gate, Hazrat Nizamuddin's Tomb, the Parliament House, Qutab Minar, etc.

Each of these tourist attractions in Delhi manifests the great history of Delhi, India.

The glorious and tumultuous history of Delhi is 5000-year-old. The history of Delhi begins with the formation of Indraprastha by the Pandavas and its subsequent conversion into a tranquil retreat. Several royal citadels such as the Indraprastha, Lal Kot, Quila Rai Pithora, Siri, Jahanpanah, Tughlakabad, Ferozabad, Dinpanah, and Delhi Sher Shahi (formerly Shahjahanabad) of various kings and emperors combine and integrate into one city that is always called Delhi. Thus, Delhi has always been identified for its power and imperial influence.

The ancient Purana Qila and the eternal Jamuna River stands witness to Delhi's historic and legendary past. The famous Red Fort, when built by Shah Jahan, drew the attention of administration towards the magnificent palaces of the fort. There were many attempts to eliminate Delhi. Nadir Shah had ordered his soldiers to plunder and annihilate Delhi. Abdali and Taimur Lane, too, tried to demolish Delhi. But the city resisted these attempts bravely and remained unshaken.

The history of Delhi encompasses the role played by the city during India's fight for independence. When India's first war of independence took place in the year 1857 AD, Delhi came to the forefront. Delhi was made the capital of India in the year 1911 by the British, which shifted all activities during the freedom struggle towards Delhi. During this period, the Azad Hind Fauz tried to capture Delhi and establish Swaraj. The popular slogan Dilli Chalo, which evolved during the freedom struggle, is still used by leaders and political parties in rallies and demonstrations.

For you to know about the History of Delhi, Indian Holiday can help you with information about the History of Delhi. Just get in touch with us for more information about History of Delhi.

Things to Do in New Delhi

Delhi Tourist Attractions

National capital state, New Delhi has got the spell to charm locals and travelers alike. Heritage lovers have Humayun's Tomb, Qutub Complex, Old Fort, Red Fort and other historic marvels carved by the mahajarajas. Shopaholics have a real reason to loosen the pockets; Palika, Sarojini Nagar, GK, Karol Bagh, Lajpat Nagar and Old Delhi. Delhi's Akshardham, India Gate, Supreme Court, Lotus Temple and Jama Masjid have set a new parameter in the brilliance of architecture.

This city/state acts as a nerve-center for nation's legitimate and political affairs. Uncountable entertainment options are offered in various malls and amusement parks of Delhi. Jama Masjid, Sri Digambar Jain Temple, Kalka Mandir, Nizamuddin Dargah, Jhandewalan Temple, Laxmi Narayan Temple and Bangla Sahib Gurudwara are magnets for pilgrims worldwide.

Foodies must get ready for a real treat for their taste-buds, as Delhi's butter chicken, daal makhani and rajma chawal are some of the food worth drooling for. In fact, talk about any state's specialty, and you can easily find it here. Delhi is fit for budget travelers, luxury travelers, kids and solo backpackers; there are a dozen of things meant for every other person who comes over.

Red Fort
A historian's paradise, Delhi is home to a phase of history that speaks out from every nook and corner of the ancient city. The memories of the glorious age of the Mughal rulers is still alive in the city, with most of their architectural glories still standing as witnesses of the era gone by. One of these is the UNESCO World Heritage Site Red Fort or the Laal Quila.

One of the most symbolic features of the Indian capital. Built by the Mughal emperor Shah Jahan around 1638 and 1648, the Red

Fort today is a busy market-place, a remembrance of Old Delhi. The Red Fort is also the site of India's national celebrations on the 15th of August, India's Independence Day.

History:

A testimony of the glorious Mughal influence on India, the Red Fort in Delhi is today is one of the important tourist attractions. The Fort, which was built by the architectural monarch Shah Jahan in 1648, was started in 1639, after which Shah Jahan changed the Mughal capital from Agra to Delhi. The inauguration of the Fort was in itself an occasion to remember with the main halls of the Fort being draped in rich fabrics brought in from fellow trading countries like China and Turkey. Designed by the renowned Mughal architects, Ustad Hamid and Ahmad, the Fort, brings to alive even today, the life of the people of the era.

Even today a visit to the Red Fort conjures images of the lives within the red sandstone walls during the golden age of the Mughals. The main point of entry, the Lahore Gate leads to the Chatta Chowk where the royalty shopped for exquisite jewelry, luxurious fabrics and other delicate artistry, where the sounds of the royal band echoes even to this day. The Meena Bazaar, one of the oldest bazaars in the world today, provides the visitors to the fort with a glimpse of the life of the commoners of the period. The elegance and regality of the Red Fort also made it one of the most coveted aspects of a conquest of India in the eyes of foreigners like Nadir Shah, who conquered the fort in 1739, depriving the Fort of a number of its treasures, including the pride of the Mughal Empire, the Peacock Throne.

Structures in Red Fort

Resplendent in her grandeur, the Red Fort is one of the most important symbols of not just India's history but also one of her greatest prides, her democracy. The Fort, built in red sandstone and one of the most prominent architectural masterpieces of the Mughal era. The medieval complex comprising of a number of palaces, offices, workshops, halls, mosques as well as market places. Built around an area of 120 acres, this UNESCO certified world heritage site consists of:

The Diwan-i-Khas or the Hall of Private Audience

Perhaps the pride of the Red Fort, the Diwan-i-Khas is today just a pale reminder of its glorious past. Decorated with precious and semi-precious stones, this was the court of the Mughal Emperor where he sat in conference with the ministers of his council. It was the former home of the heavily ornamented Peacock Throne.

The Diwan-i-Amn or the Hall of Public Audience

It is the court in which the emperor addressed the pleas of his citizens. The rectangular hall has three aisles and nine multiple arches, which housed the royal throne beneath a marble canopy decorated with precious stones and floral motifs.

The Rang Mahal (Palace of Colors) or the Imtiaz Mahal

Consisting of six apartments divided by arched pillars constructed in a typically Mughal style of architecture, this beautiful palace is built over a basement that in turn is built around a main hall with rooms at each end.

The Khas Mahal (Private Palace)

The emperor's personal palace, this exotic structure consisted of the following chambers:

- The Taasbikhana (Chamber of Telling Beads)
- The Khwabgah (Sleeping Chamber)
- Baithak (Sitting Room)
- Muthamman Burj or Jharokah-i-Darshan (Showing Balcony)

The other notable structures of the Red Fort are:

- The Moti Masjid or the Pearl Mosque
- The Hayat-Baksh Bagh or the Life-giving Garden
- Zafar Mahal
- The Hamam or the Bath

Though the Red Fort is but a faint image of its former glory today, it still manages to hold its visitors spell-bound with images of its regal charm. Light and sound shows are arranged at the fort that is sure to transport you to the medieval era of the Mughals. Tickets for the show which are organized in Hindi as well as in English can be bought from the Fort.

India Gate

Located in Rajpath, perhaps the most prestigious area in the entirety of the city of Delhi, the India Gate was built to commemorate the death of 90,000 India soldiers, who were killed in the North West Province during the First World War and the Afghan Conquest of 1919. Constructed in sandstone and rising to a height of 160 ft., the height of the arch is 136' externally and 87'6" internally. India Gate is also credited for being the first gate to be constructed in New Delhi. The names of the soldiers in whose memory the Gate was constructed is inscribed on its walls, beside which an eternal flame called the

Amar Jawan Jyoti. The foundation stone of the memorial was laid by HRH the Duke of Connaught in 1921 and the monument was dedicated to the nation 10 years later by the then Viceroy, Lord Irwin. The Amar Jawan Jyoti was added to the memorial after India had gained her independence, in memory of the soldiers of the Indo-Pakistan War of December 1971.

Today, the India Gate is one of the most important symbols of India, being at the center of the itinerary of most of the tourists who visit the country's capital city. Whether it is eating out at the roadside eateries or enjoying a monkey show outside, India Gate offers entertainment for everyone. So in case you are planning a trip to the capital, make sure India Gate plays a pivotal role in your itinerary.

History:

Situated at the eastern end of Rajpath in Central Delhi is the 42 m high stone arch of victory, renowned as the India Gate. Formally known as the All India War Memorial previously, the foundation stone of this magnanimous structure was laid by the Duke of Connaught in 1921 and dedicated to the nation in 1931 by the then Viceroy, Lord Irwin.

Designed by Sir Edwin Lutyens, the India Gate stands on a low base of red Bharatpur stone and rises in stages to a huge cornice. Above on both sides is inscribed INDIA, flanked by MCM and to the right, XIX. The names of the 90,000 soldiers of the Indian Army who lost their lives in World War-I, and an additional 13,516 names who sacrificed their lives in the North-West Frontier in the Afghan War of 1919 are inscribed on the walls of this grand construction.

In order to honor the numerous unknown gallant soldiers who died fighting for the country, an eternal flame or Amar Jawan Jyoti was lit under the arch of India Gate in 1971. Uniformed soldiers stand guard over the flame. As a tribute to these dead soldiers, a shining rifle crowned by a soldier's helmet is placed on a high pedestal near the flame.

Annual Event:

Situated at the eastern end of Rajpath in Central Delhi is the 42 m high stone arch of victory, renowned as the India Gate. This magnificent edifice was constructed in 1931 in memory of the Indian soldiers who lost their lives in the battlefield. Following are the special annual events that take place at India Gate

Republic Day Parade

Every year on 26th January, the day celebrated as the Republic Day of India, the Indian President places a wreath at the eternal flame Amar Jawan Jyoti under the arch of India Gate to pay his respects to the Indian armed forces who laid down their lives for the sake of the country. It is followed by a grand parade that moves along Rajpath, which comprise of marching contingents, tanks and weaponry, vibrant floats, folk dances and school children from different parts of India who participate in this colorful ceremony.

Swar Utsav

This three-day musical extravaganza is organized by the Delhi Tourism every October on the luxuriant lawns of the India Gate. The music lovers are kept enthralled by the performance of the best Indian classical musicians during this event.

Fast - Facts:

The 42 m high stone arch of victory, renowned as the India Gate, was constructed in 1931 in memory of the Indian soldiers who lost their lives in the battlefield. Following are some fast facts about India Gate.

Location

Less than a mile from Connaught Place, (Rajeev Chowk) at the eastern end of Rajpath in Central Delhi.

Best Time to Visit

Open on all days of the year, round the clock, but preferably be there between 7.00 pm-9.30 pm. There is no admission fee, as it is open to all. It requires approximately an hour to look around this majestic edifice.

How to Reach

To reach the India Gate, you can fly down to the Indira Gandhi International Airport in Delhi. You can either avail of local buses from various points within the city to reach the monument, or hire auto-rickshaws and taxis or take the metro rail. The nearest functional Metro station is Kendriya Terminal, while the nearest railway station is the New Delhi Railway Station.

Nearby Places to Eat

Some of the popular eat-outs near India Gate are Hotel Le Meridien, Imperial Hotel, Hotel Inter-Continental, Parikrama Revolving restaurant, etc.

Nearby Attractions:

Situated at the eastern end of Rajpath in Central Delhi is the 42 m high stone arch of victory, renowned as the India Gate. This magnificent edifice was constructed in 1931 in memory of the Indian soldiers who lost their lives in the battlefield. Following are the other tourist attractions near India Gate:

- **Rashtrapati Bhawan:** The official residence of the Indian President.
- **North and South Block:** All important government offices are located here
- **Parliament House:** The place where the Indian Parliament meets and the world's largest democracy functions.
- **National Museum:** The museum has an extensive collection of historical artifacts, both of Indian and foreign origin.
- **National Gallery of Modern Art:** Famous for its contemporary Indian art collection, the museum exhibits around 4,000 paintings, graphics, and sculptures of modern artists.
- **Connaught Place:** This popular market offers everything from jewelry, books, art, leather goods and Indian and international clothes.
- **Central Cottage Industries Emporium:** Stores Indian handicrafts and curios.

> <u>Baba Kharak Singh Marg</u>: This market houses each state's exclusive art and craft created by traditional and accomplished artisans.

Humayun's Tomb

The Humayun's Tomb is one of the UNESCO World Heritage Site in Delhi, India's capital city. One of the inspirational architecture of its time, the design and layout has inspired many similar structures. Built in the memory of Humayun, by his Persian widow, Haji Begum, it was the first architectural construction built during Akbar's reign.

Built around 1562-1572 AD, Humayun's Tomb is one of the leading attractions of Delhi today, drawing thousands of visitors every day. Exhibiting a very obvious influence of Persian architecture that owes its origin to its Persian architect Mirak Mirza Ghiyuath, the mausoleum was built on the banks of the Yamuna River, next to the shrine of Sufi saint of Chisti Silsilah, Nizamuddin Auliya. A number of other Mughal luminaries are buried here like - Hamida Begum, Akbar's mother, Dara Shikoh, Shah Jahan's son and Bahadur Shah II, the last Mughal Emperor

The garden tomb, is in the UNESCO's list of World Heritage Sites for the architectural value and cultural significance. It is under the ownership of the Archaeological Survey of India. The tomb is an architectural masterpiece forming the basis of the definition of Mughal architecture that is characterized by high arches and double domes. The Tomb is maintained by the Aga Khan Trust that has to a large extent restored its lost glory to the tomb.

History:

Much of the tourist attractions of Delhi surround the history of the Mughal dynasty, most of whom have shaped India as we see her today. One of these rulers is the charming and charismatic Mughal emperor Humayun, a capable ruler, whose life was tragically cut short by a freak accident when he fell down the stairs of the Sher Mandal Library. Built in memory of this charismatic ruler, the history of Humayun's Tomb is an important part of the history of India as well as the history of Delhi.

The tomb was built in the memory of Humayun by his Persian widow Haji Begum who planned the architecture of the tomb after consulting with one of the most notable architects of her homeland, Mirak Mirza Ghiyuath. The architecture, which showcases a very prominent influence of the Persian style of architecture, is credited to be the first and the most important architectural endeavor of the reign of Emperor Akbar, often regarded to be the greatest of all the Mughal emperors.

One of the most important factors that have added to the claim to fame of the Humayun's Tomb is the fact that the architecture of the tomb has been one of the greatest influences in the architecture of one of the Seven Wonders of the World, the Taj Mahal.

ISKCON Temple

Raja Dhirshain Marg, Sant Nagar, near the East of Kailash locality, ISKCON Temple in Delhi is one of the 40 temples in India that belongs to the International Society for Krishna Consciousness, dedicated to Lord Krishna. A part of the Hare Krishna Movement was started by Acharya Bhaktivedanta Swami Prabhupada. The devotees and followers of the Hare Rama Hare Krishna cult built this temple in 1998 to disseminate the message of the Bhagwad Gita.

Features of ISKCON Temple in Delhi

ISKCON Temple in Delhi is an artistic splendor. The interior walls of the temple have been decorated with aesthetic works of

Russian artists representing the different phases of life of various deities like Radha-Krishan, and Sita-Ram.

The main attraction of ISKCON Temple in Delhi is its central prayer hall and the temple museum. Treat your eyes with the wonderfully sculpted idols of Radha-Krishna with other deities present in the central hall with informative religious lines and shibboleths.

Another attraction of ISKCON Temple in Delhi is the temple museum. The museum organizes multimedia shows. It not only helps the devotees understand the story of the epics Ramayana and Mahabharata, but also gives a brief interpretative understanding of views, philosophy and practice of the Hare Krishna cult. Don't miss this is an interesting feature of ISKCON Temple in Delhi.

Annual Events:

There is a special delight in visiting the ISKCON Temple in Delhi during one of its festive season.

The festival of Janmashtami at ISKCON Temple in Delhi

Janmashtami, the birth of Lord Krishna is celebrated at ISKCON Temple in Delhi. The gala event falls in the month of August or

September during which the religious activities and enthusiasm of the devotees in the temple are at their highest level. Thousands of devotees at ISKCON Temple in Delhi visit on this auspicious day and the atmosphere of joyous celebration is truly exhilarating.

The Other Events at ISKCON Temple

Religious programs at ISKCON Temple in Delhi include:

- Kirtan
- Aarti
- Pravachan

The museum at ISKCON Temple in Delhi organizes regular shows in the evening at nominal charges on all days except Monday.

Fast - Facts:

Location: temple located on Raja Dhirshain Marg, Sant Nagar, near the eastern side of Kailash locality

- ✓ <u>Well Known For</u>: Radha Krishna Temple
- ✓ <u>Time to visit</u>: Open on all days
- ✓ <u>How to Reach</u>: Tourists can either avail buses from different points or can take auto rickshaws, taxis or metro to reach the temple

- ✓ <u>Nearest Railway Station</u>: Nizamuddin Railway Station
- ✓ <u>Nearest Metro station</u>: Central Secretariat
- ➢ <u>Nearest International Airport</u>: Indira Gandhi International Airport

Nearby Attractions:

ISKCON Temple is a famous pilgrim destination which records a considerable amount of footfall. Surrounding this religious hub is a number of attractive tourist spots like:

<u>Kalkaji Temple</u>-The temple of Goddess Kali, situated on a hill top and a major pilgrimage place during Navratri. Legend goes that the founder of this temple is a farmer. Built in the 18th century it is hardly a kilometer away from Okhla Industrial Estate and Nehru Palace.

<u>Nizamuddin's shrine</u>- Located in Nizamuddin village, situated close to the Humayun's tomb, not far away from the Eastern end of the Lodi Road is the shrine of the famous Muslim Sufi saint, Sheikh Hazrat Nizamuddin Aulia Chishti.

<u>Khirki Masjid</u>- Situated just 2 kilometers away from Qutab Minar, in the center of Khirki Village, is the khirki Masjid or Mosque. It is a fine example of 'closed mosque' in North India. The

outstanding feature of this mosque is its window opening with jalis or tracery, thereby naming then latticed windows.

<u>Chirag-i-Dihli's Dargah</u>- It is the tomb of Sufi saint Nasir-ud-Din Mahmud who was also known as Raushan Chirag-i-Dihli. Located in the Chirag Delhi Village, the place can be reached by taking the Lal Bahadur Shastri Marg through the Chirag main road or one can also take the Outer Ring Road through the Soami Nagar south colony.

Some of the famous food joints and eateries serving eclectic dishes are completely vegetarian restaurant within the temple complex, named Govinda Restaurant. Other names include Hotel Park Royal, Karim's.

Nearby Shopping Venues include Nehru Place, C R Park Market and Kalkaji Market.

Qutab Minar
Qutub Minar, a UNESCO World Heritage Site is the highest stone tower in India. The construction of the Qutub Minar was started by Qutub-ud-Din Aibak in 1199 and was finished by his successor and son-in-law, Iltutmish. This magnificent structure was named after the Sufi saint, Khwaja Qutubuddin Bakhtiyar Kaki. Though

the exact purpose of the Qutub Minar is not known but it is believed that it served as a minaret to the adjoining mosque and was used by the muezzins to call the faithful to prayer.

Description

Constructed in red and buff sandstone and covered with intricate carvings and verses from the Holy Quran, Qutub Minar has five stories surrounded by a projected balcony and buttressed by stone brackets, which are decked with honeycomb designs. The Qutub Minar is 72.5m high and there are 379 steps. The diameter of the base is 14.3m while the top floor's diameter measures 2.7m.

There are numerous inscriptions on the Qutub Minar in Arabic and Nagari characters. The inscriptions contain information on the work done on the Qutub Minar by different rulers like Firoz Shah Tughlaq, Sikandar Lodi, as well as by Major R. Smith. It was built on the ruins of Lal Kot, the Red Citadel in the city of Dhillika, the capital of the Tomar and Chauhana Rajputs, the last Hindu rulers of Delhi.

There are many other remarkable buildings and structures in the Qutub Minar complex, including the Quwwat-ul-Islam mosque, the first mosque built in India. It was constructed by Qutub-ud-din Aibak using materials of 27 Jain and Hindu temples. There is also the famous Alai Darwaza at the entrance of the Quwwat-ul-Islam mosque, built by Ala-ud-din Khilji. To the west of the Quwwat-ul-Islam mosque is the tomb of Iltutmish. Close to the mosque is the 4th century Iron pillar, one of Delhi's most interesting structures.

History:

A glance at this tall imposing tower of Delhi called the Qutub Minar will give you the details about its history. This red and buff colored sandstone structure of Qutub Minar has a unique towering presence. It's considered to be the tallest tower of India.

The foundation of Qutub Minar was laid by Qutubuddin Aibak in 1193 and it was completed by Illtutmish and then Firoz Shah Tughluq in 1368. Built of red sandstone, one can witness the stark differences in architecture of different periods and different dynasties.

The monument located near Mehrauli rises to a height of 237.8 ft. It has a series of 399 steps to reach the topmost level. When Qutubuddin Aibak was crowned the king he wanted to celebrate the victory of Islam and the fall of the Hindu empire. So he built this tower to establish the supremacy of the Islam over the Hindu monarchy.

The high standing tower has shafts and balconies and the walls are adorned with inscribed verses from Quran. Intricate carvings lend an exquisite look to the minaret. There are inscriptions that tell us the history of Qutub Minar.

The tall column of red stone has been a silent witness to the changing dynasties and passing time. The meaning of the word Qutub Minar is "axis minaret". The first three stories of the tower are made of red sandstone by Qutubuddin Aibak and Iltutmish and the last two stories are made of marble by Firoz Shah Tughluq. The Quwwat-ul-Islam mosque is located near the minaret. It is considered to be one of the oldest mosques in India.

Purana Qila - Old Fort

Apart from being the capital of India, Delhi is a fascinating city with pleasant contradictions. Comprising of Old Delhi and New Delhi, the city is home to famous tourist destinations like the Laxmi Narayan Temple, India Gate, Jama Masjid, Red Fort, Qutub Minar, Humayun's Tomb, and the vivacious shopping bazaar of Chandni Chowk. One such tourist attraction in Delhi is the Old

Fort, also known as Purana Qila in Hindi, one of the most famous monuments in Delhi, India.

Background

The founder of the Sur Dynasty, Sher Shah Suri, constructed this enormous fort in the 16th-century to defend his most prized possession, Delhi, from the Mughals. In 1539-40, he defeated his arch-rival, Mughal emperor Humayun, in two consecutive battles and nearly brought an end to the Mughal Empire in India by capturing two Mughal strongholds - Delhi and Agra. Though the Purana Qila has not been witness to any major battle, its very existence kept the Mughals away from invading Delhi. But after Sher Shah Suri died in 1545, Humayun recaptured Delhi and Agra with the help of Persians.

Humayun made good use of the octagonal red sandstone tower known as Sher Mandal as his library and observatory. Some Mughal historical documents suggest that Humayun died as a result of the injuries he suffered after falling down from the steps of the Sher Mandal. It is being said that the Mughals considering the fort to be a cursed one after the death of the Humayun, and vacated the edifice. As a consequence, the Mughals had to construct a new fort to defend Delhi from foreign invasions. This fort was named Lal Qila, popular known as Red Fort.

Description

The unique Mughal-Hindu-Afghan architecture of the fort not only attracts tourists from world over, but has also drawn attention of archaeologists and Indian historians. Recent archaeological excavations have exposed evidences of pottery and other pieces of art and handicrafts which throw a new light on the existence of Indraprastha, a historic city mentioned in the great epic Mahabharata. A report by the Archaeological Survey of India suggests that Indraprastha stood on the site where the Old Fort stands today.

The historic structure of the Purana Qila, that has stood witness to the periods of anarchy, the rise and fall of empires in Delhi, presently houses the Delhi Zoo, Delhi's largest zoological park, and a Boat club.

Excavations at Purana Qila

The Purana Quila or Old Fort in Delhi was built by Mughal Emperor Humayun and Sher Shah Suri in the sixteenth century. Legend has it that the site where Humayun erected his fort was once known as Indraparastha, the capital of the Pandavas of the Mahabharata. Though this information cannot be confirmed, excavations at Purana Quila have shown that there thrived a prosperous civilization at this place suring the 1000 BC. The earliest houses belonged to about the forth century B.C. In fact, till the end of the nineteenth century, there was a village called Indarpat (which sounds very similar to 'Indraprastha') inside the fort. Was ancient Indraprastha located here? This is a question that is difficult to answer with a simple 'yes' or 'no.'

Purana Qila

The excavations at Purana Qila tell us about the lives of people who lived here hundreds of years ago. Houses made of sun-dried bricks as well as bricks baked in kilns, terracotta figurines of humans and animals, a special kind of shiny pottery that archaeologists call Northern Black Polished Ware and Painted Grey Ware were some of the artefacts excavated. Lots of seals and coins were discovered too. The houses found here had drains which carried waste water into soak pits dug into the ground. Terracotta ring wells reflecting their clever architectural skills were also found. An interesting find was a jug containing bells, ghunghroos (anklets with bells), and various objects of copper. In about the forth century A.D., the settlement at the

Purana Qila seems to have started to decline. Houses at this time were made out of reused bricks of earlier buildings. Many centuries later, in the tenth century, a fortification wall was built around the settlement.

In the sixteenth century, the Mughal king Humayun built his fort at this place and forever buried the remains of a civilization that once thrived on the expertise and skills of an enterprising populace.

Fast- Facts:

The Purana Quila or Old Fort in Delhi was built by Mughal Emperor Humayun and Sher Shah Suri in the sixteenth century. The fortification wall was built by Humayun and the rest by Sher Shah. In 1539-40, Sher Shah Suri defeated his arch-rival, Mughal emperor Humayun, in two consecutive battles and nearly brought an end to the Mughal Empire in India by capturing two Mughal strongholds - Delhi and Agra. He constructed this enormous fort in the 16th-century to defend his most prized possession, Delhi, from the Mughals. Though the massive Purana Qila has not been witness to any major battle, its very existence kept the Mughals away from invading Delhi. After his death

Humayun recaptured Delhi with aid from the Persians. Below is a list of Fast Facts on Purana Qila for your convenience.

Location- the Purana Qila is located on the eastern side of India Gate and north of Humayun's tomb on Mathura Road. Also Known as- Old Fort.

Best Time to Visit- early morning or just before sundown.

Entry- INR 5 for Indian citizens and INR 100 for foreigners.

Photography Fees- Rs. 25/-

Mode of Transport- auto rickshaws, buses and taxis are available from different parts of Delhi.

Nearest terminals- the nearest railway station is New Delhi staion, nearest airport Indira Gandhi airport and nearest metro station Connaught Place.

Nearest City Landmark- Connaught Place, the heart of New Delhi is very near and is the hub of the best eateries, shops and markets.

Nearby Attractions:

The Purana Quila or Old Fort in Delhi was built by Mughal Emperor Humayun and Sher Shah Suri in the sixteenth century. The fortification wall was built by Humayun and the rest by Sher Shah. In 1539-40, Sher Shah Suri defeated his arch-rival, Mughal emperor Humayun, in two consecutive battles and nearly brought an end to the Mughal Empire in India by capturing two Mughal strongholds - Delhi and Agra. He constructed this enormous fort in the 16th-century to defend his most prized possession, Delhi, from the Mughals. Though the massive Purana Qila has not been witness to any major battle, its very existence kept the Mughals away from invading Delhi. After his death Humayun recaptured Delhi with aid from the Persians. Below is a list of nearby tourist attractions to Purana Qila.

Qila-i-kuhna Masjid-

Built by Sher Shah Suri in 1541, this mosque is one of the most fascinating buildings inside the Purana Qila.

Delhi Zoo-

Established in 1959, this is considered one of the finest zoos in Asia and is housed inside the Purana Qila. It also has a boat club.

Light and Sound Show-

The Delhi Tourism organizes a light and sound show inside the old fort after 5 pm and before 9 pm.

Humayun's Tomb-

Built in 1570, this is the first garden tomb of the Indian subcontinent and has been declared a UNESCO world heritage site.

India Gate-

Originally called the War Memorial Arch, India Gate commemorates the Indian soldiers who sacrificed their lives during the First World War. On its walls are inscribed the names of 60,000 men who fell fighting for the British Empire.

Buddha Jayanti Park

Buddha Jayanti Park is a beautiful well manicured garden with sprawling lawns and blooming flowers. Though relatively new in the list of parks in Delhi, it is quite popular amongst Delhites and tourists alike. This garden was built to commemorate the 2500 year of Lord Buddha's attainment of Nirvana. The significance of the garden lies in the fact that sapling of the original Bodhi tree (under which Buddha attained Nirvana) has been brought all the way from Sri Lanka and transplanted here. Emperor Asoka's daughter Sanghamitra took a sapling from the original Bodhi tree in Bodh Gaya and went to Sri Lanka to preach Buddhism. Check out the beautiful idol of Buddha that lies at one corner of the park. Buddha Garden Delhi features as one of the most coveted Tourist attractions in New Delhi.

Buddha Jayanti Park is a hotspot for young couples too. Buddha Jayanti or Buddha Purnima is celebrated each may here with great aplomb. This park was dedicated to the 14th Dalai Lama in 1993.

Fast - Facts:

Location: Near Delhi Ridge Road

Accessibility: Near to Rajiv Chowk Metro station

Time Required: 1 hour

Open On: All days from 5 AM to 7 PM

Admission Fee: Nil

Nearby Attractions:

If you are visiting Buddha Jayanti Park, we recommend you to stop by at all the other nearby attractions around Buddha Jayanti Park. Situated at an equi distance from some other interesting places worth visiting, Buddha Jayanti Park serves as a base wherein you can start to plan your trips ahead for the day. Make an early start since the park opens at the wee hours of the morning. Some of the Nearby attractions to Buddha Jayanti Park are :

Talkatora Gardens:

This beautiful garden has a historical significance. The Marathas were defeated here by the Mughals in 1738. Significantly enough the garden derived its name from the water tank that was one of the major attraction of this place.

Shaped like a large swimming pool, the tank and garden proves to be a pleasant respite for the world weary travelers and localites alike. The well maintained gardens and blooming flowers are a balm to the sore eyes. Horticulture shows are organized here. Likewise many children shows and cultural programs are organized in the vicinity of the park.

Cathedral of the Sacred Heart.

This church stretching over 14 acres of land is another nearby attractions to Buddha Jayanti Park. Located near Gol Dak Khana, New Delhi, this is one of the main Catholic Church in New Delhi. The main moral of the church lies in the universal brotherhood of man and humanity. In 1929, the archbishop of Agra laid the foundation of the Church.

Jantar Mantar:

This geometrical structure lies at the very heart of Delhi near Connaught place. It was constructed to keep track of the different celestial bodies in the days of yore.

India Gate:

This monumental gate was constructed to commemorate the 90,000 Indian soldiers who laid their lives in First World War.

Parks and temples, monuments and museums, ruins and forts all these culminate to make Delhi what it is- a perfect blend of old and new. Tourist attractions in New Delhi are many and varied.

National Science Center

The National Science Centre in Delhi is popular among children. The Museum houses a unique collection of science models to arouse interest among children. The children are made aware of the effective use of science in our lives. The museum is all about learning and having fun. National Science Centre in Delhi is located on the main Bhairon Road in front of Gate no.1 of Pragati Maidan. It is one of the best science centres of National Council of Science Museum (NCSM) exhibiting scientific models and intriguing artifacts.

Several galleries in the centre pertaining to various themes have a plethora of exhibits. These exhibits are based on different laws and theories of science. The students are made to understand these theories with the help of live demonstrations. The scientific models on display at the Human Biology Gallery are interesting. Dinosaur's gallery of animals of Mesozoic era is popular among children. A number of exhibits showcase India's contribution to Science and mathematics, about Nobel Prize winners and exponents of the field. The centre encloses a well stocked library, a planetarium and a cyber school which hosts several courses for students as well as teachers. A souvenir shop within the complex sells key chains, t-shirts and chinaware. National Science Center in Delhi is a fascinating museum. Tourists must visit the museum to gain insightful perspectives on scientific laws and theories.

Annual Events:

National Science Centre in Delhi is a popular museum among children. The intriguing artifacts develop curiosity in children. Various displays highlight scientific laws and theories. The museum involves a learning experience along with fun. The Center hosts several annual events. It is one of the best science centres of National Council of Science Museum (NCSM) exhibiting scientific models The Annual events in National Science Center in Delhi make for a learning experience.

The Centre organizes interactive sessions with the leading scientists of the country. Young students enjoy the science picnics organized in groups. It is an occasion of fun and a learning experience.

Fast - Facts:

Location:

In front of Gate no-1, Bhairon Road, Pragati Maidan, Delhi

Special Features:

Library, a planetarium and a cyber school, a souvenir shop

How to Reach:

Tourists can avail of local buses, auto rickshaws, taxi and metro rail in order to reach the national science center in Delhi

Nearest International Airport: Indira Gandhi International Airport

Nearest Metro Station: Pragati Maidan

Functional Metro Station: Central Secretariat

Nearest Railway Station: Nizamuddin Railway Station

Open: On all days, 10:00 A.M to 5:30 p.m.

Nearby Attractions:

National Science Center in Delhi is one of the best museums in Delhi that provides a deep insight into scientific laws and theories. The center is popular among children. The Center is home to an exotic collection of scientific models to develop interest among children. Tourists thronging Delhi must visit the National Science Center which entails a learning experience with fun. You can also visit the fascinating nearby attractions of National Science Center in Delhi to enjoy a wholesome experience on tours to Delhi. The nearby attractions of national Science Center in Delhi are Pragati Maidan, Craft Museum, Nila Gumbad on southeastern side, Purana Qila, Delhi Zoo, Sabz Burz, Nili Chhatri, India Gate, Ashokan Rock Edict, Nizam-ud-din's Shrine and Khairul Manzil Masjid.

Pragati Maidan: Pragati Maidan is an exhibition centre located in the center of the capital city. Pragati Maidan plays host to several International and National Trade Fairs.

Craft Museum: It preserves intriguing artifacts and curios of western origin. 20,000 items of folk and tribal arts and crafts are preserved in a concrete, but almost 'invisible' building.

Nila Gumbad: Nila Gumbad is an architectural marvel built by Mughal emperor Humayun.

Purana Qila: Purana Qila or old fort was built by Humayun and completed by Sher Shah in the 16th century. Legend has it that the ancient city of Indraprastha existed here. Potteries like painted grey-ware have been discovered here. Excavations during 1970's and 1980's have revealed that the mound within the fort was inhabited from 1000 B.C.

Delhi Zoo: The National zoological park of Delhi or the Delhi zoo is located adjacent to the Purana Qila. It shelters over thousand varieties of mammals, reptiles and avian species.

Sabz Burz: An architectural splendor built by Humayun.

Nili Chhatri: It is believed to be the tomb of Naubat Khan, a noble man of Akbar's court.

India Gate: 42m stone arch of victory is a memorial of 90,000 martyrs of the First World War.

Ashokan Rock Edict: Discovered in 1966, the Ashokan rock edict is a pointer to the fact that Delhi was an important commercial town in the Mauryan era and a connecting link between major provinces of North India.

Nizam-ud-din's Shrine: Located near Humayun's tomb, it is the famous shrine of the sufi saint Nizam-ud-din.

Khairul Manzil Masjid: It is a holy mosque near the Purana Qila and Delhi zoo entrance. It is considered as one of the auspicious houses.

The Nearby Places to Eat are Sweet Corner, Nathu's (both in Sunder Nagar Market), Hotel Oberoi, Flavors of Defence colony, Indian Habitat Center in Lodi Road, Nizamuddin's Karim and roadside food stalls.

Shopping lovers can visit the Nearby Shopping Centers of Sunder Nagar Market Connaught Place, Central Cottage Industries Janpath and Palika Bazaar.

Nizamuddin's Tomb

Located in the heart of the historic Nizammuddin Village about 2 kms away from Humayun's Tomb is Nizammuddin's Tomb, one of the country's most revered places and also an important tourist attraction of Delhi.

The tomb which is the shrine of the famous humanitarian Muslim Sufi and mystic saint, Sheikh Hazrat Nizamuddin Aulia Chishti is one of the most respected places of worship in the country. Revered equally amongst both Hindus as well as Muslims of the country, the mausoleum as we see it today was built in 1562 by a rich merchant called Faridu'n Khan.

Born in the city of Badaun in Uttar Pradesh in 1236, Sheikh Hazrat Nizamuddin was the disciple and successor of the saint

Sheikh Farid Shakarganj and commanded a large following of devotees which included names like Alauddin Khilji, Mohammed bin Tughlaq and the great poet Amir Khusrau. Even Mughal emperors like Babur, Humayun, Akbar, Jahangir, and Shah Jahan stopped to seek the blessings of the Sufi saint at his shrine, every time their processions crossed his sacred Dargah. Though the original shrine no longer exists, yet, the site is still considered to be one of the holiest shrines of the country and never ceases to attract thousands of devotees each year.

Today, the shrine also includes a mosque and tombs of many other famous people who wished to be buried near its sacred grounds. The architectural prowess of Shahjahan too graces this landmark, with marble arches and a majestic marble pavilion being added to the shrine. The devotees who throng this place tie red threads on the lattice screens or jails to indicate the fulfillment of their wishes. It is customary to visit the shrine during the period of the Festival of Urs which is held twice a year to commemorate the anniversaries of Hazrat Nizamuddin Aulia and the renowned poet Amir Khusrau. Besides this, Thursday Evening is considered to be the most pious time of the year to visit the shrine when millions of people from all across the city throng to the mausoleum to seek the blessings of this great Sufi saint.

History:

Situated in the historic Nizamuddin village is the shrine of a famous humanitarian Muslim Sufi and mystic saint, Sheikh Hazrat Nizamuddin Aulia Chishti. Born at Badaun in Uttar Pradesh in 1236 AD, he was the disciple of saint Sheikh Farid Shakarganj, who appointed him as his successor. Mughal Emperors like Babur, Humayun, Akbar, Jahangir, and Shah Jahan paid their reverence at the sacred Dargah, halting their procession. People of all faiths venerated the saint, who was popular because of his doctrine of renunciation and tolerance towards other religions. Hazrat Nizamuddin died in 1325 and his shrine today is a renowned pilgrimage site.

The original tomb of Hazrat Nizamuddin no longer exists. The present structure was constructed by a nobleman named Faridun Khan in the mid-15th century. It was renovated and decorated by Firoz Shah Tughlaq, as well as by later rulers. It has a marble-paved courtyard where the sacred shrine of the saint can be seen. Shah Jahan later added the majestic pavilion with its marble arches and lattice screens known as jalis. Worshippers tie red threads to these jalis as signs of wishes they hope will be fulfilled. The roof, presumably constructed by Akbar II, is crested by a dome decked by vertical black stripes. The main grave is wrapped with a scented dark green colored cloth.

Structures Hazrat Nizamuddin's Tomb

Following are some of the famous structures near Hazrat Nizamuddin's Tomb -

Jamat Khana Masjid

Located west of Nizamuddin's tomb in the same complex, Jamat Khana Masjid is one of the oldest structures in the whole region, built in 1325. It consists of three bays, each crowned by a low dome.

Tombs of Jahanara, Mohammed Shah and Mirza Jahangir

The tomb of Jahanara, the favorite daughter of Shah Jahan, is located south of the sacred shrine of the saint. The tomb of Mohammed Shah, who was once the emperor of Delhi, also lies within the enclosure. Another tomb, which lies nearby, is the tomb of Mirza Jahangir, the eldest son of Akbar II.

Baoli

A large sacred Baoli or stepped well, built by Hazrat Nizamuddin himself, is positioned near the northern gate of the enclosure of the Dargah.

Chini-ka-Burj and Bai-Kodaldai's Tomb

There is a small mosque Chini-ka-Burj on the western wall of the baoli with three compartments, each with an arched opening. Just near the baoli is Bai-Kodalai's tomb, a small marble pavilion with three arched entrances and vaulted roof.

Tomb of Amir Khusrau

The tomb of Amir Khusrau, the eminent saint and poet in the reign of Alauddin Khilji, lies at the southern end of the main enclosure, crowded with the tombs of princes and nobles.

Fast - Facts:

Fast facts about Hazrat Nizamuddin's Tomb Situated in the historic Nizamuddin village is the shrine of a famous humanitarian Muslim Sufi and mystic saint, Sheikh Hazrat Nizamuddin Aulia Chishti. Following are some fast facts about Hazrat Nizamuddin's Tomb -

Location

About 2 kilometers away from Humayun's tomb at the eastern end of Lodi Road and near Mathura Road in Central Delhi.

Time to Visit

Open on all days of the year, round the clock, but preferably be there on Thursday evenings between 5-7 pm, when the place comes alive with flowers, prayer caps, and religious items. There is no admission fee, as it is open to all. It requires approximately 2½ hours looking around this grand structure.

How to Reach

To reach the Hazrat Nizamuddin's Tomb, you can fly down to the Indira Gandhi International Airport in Delhi. You can either avail of local buses from various points within the city to reach the monument, or hire auto-rickshaws and taxis or take the metro rail. The nearest functional Metro station is Central Secretariat, while the nearest railway station is the Nizamuddin Railway Station.

Nearby Places to Eat

Some of the popular eat-outs near Hazrat Nizamuddin's Tomb are Hotel Oberoi, Sweet Corner, Nathu's, Flavors, Eatopia, etc. Also be at Karim's, famous for kebabs.

Nearby Attractions:

Following are some of the tourist attractions near Hazrat Nizamuddin's Tomb -

Atgah Khan's Tomb: This tomb lies in the northeast of the main enclosure of Nizamuddin's sacred shrine.

Mirza Ghalib's Tomb: Located north of the enclosure of Chaunsath Khamba, this tomb is close to the Nizamuddin shrine.

Chaunsath Khamba: Comprising of 64 pillars, this structure is located just behind Mirza Ghalib's tomb.

Nila Gumbad: An impressive tomb made of blue tiles and stone.

Purana Qila: An enormous 16th-century fort constructed by Sher Shah Suri to defend Delhi from the Mughals.

Delhi Zoo: Located next to Purana Qila, the zoo houses varieties of animals, reptiles and birds.

Sabz Burz: A blue colored Baghdadi tomb, an octagonal structure.

Nili Chhatri: This octagonal edifice is placed on the compound of the Delhi Public School.

India Gate: This monument was constructed in memory of the Indian soldiers who lost their lives in the battlefield.

Ashokan Rock Edict: This famous engraved slanted rock-face of the Ashokan period is situated on the main Raja Dhirshain Marg.

Khairul Manzil Masjid: This 16th-century structure was built by Maham Anga, an influential wet nurse of the Emperor Akbar.

Sunder Nagar Market: Popular for antiques, jewelry, and brassware

Lajpat Nagar Market: An ideal hub for garments

Dilli Haat: This market houses some excellent handicrafts and ethnic items.

Parliament House

Apart from being the capital of India, Delhi is a fascinating city with pleasant contradictions. Comprising of Old Delhi and New Delhi, the city is home to famous tourist destinations like the Laxmi Narayan Temple, India Gate, Jama Masjid, Red Fort, Qutub Minar, Humayun's Tomb, and the vivacious shopping bazaar of Chandni Chowk. One such tourist attraction in Delhi is the Parliament House, the place where the Indian Parliament meets and the world's largest democracy functions.

Background

It was the Montagu-Chelmsford reforms of 1919 that gave birth to the Parliament House. Earlier called the Circular House, it was added to the layout at a later stage following the reforms which created a large Legislative Assembly. This is the reason for the Parliament House being also called Sansad Bhawan, which means a large Legislative Assembly.

A brainchild of Herbert Baker, this magnanimous structure was much criticized in comparison with Lutyens creations. In January 1931, an article by Robert Byron in Architectural Review describes it thus - "The Council Chamber has been Sir Herbert's unhappiest venture. Its effect from a distance has been described. It resembles a Spanish bull-ring, lying like a mill-wheel dropped accidentally on its side."

Description

The massive, spherical building of the Parliament House comprises of three semicircular chambers for the Legislatures and a Central Library crowned by a 27.4m high dome. The dome is 173m in diameter and covers 2.02 hectares in area, enclosed by a verandah with 144 columns. The three semi-circular areas were designed for the Chamber of Princes, the Council of State and the Legislative Assembly. Today they house the chambers of the Lok Sabha (House of the People), Rajya Sabha (Upper House) and the library. The boundary wall has blocks of sandstone carved in geometrical patterns that reflect the Mughal jalis.

Location and entrance

The Parliament House is situated on the northwest of Vijay Chowk, next to the Secretariat buildings at the end of the Parliament Street (Sansad Marg), New Delhi, India. Entrance to outsiders is not allowed without official permission, whether Parliament is in session or not. To obtain a visitor's pass to Sansad Bhawan, Indian nationals should apply to the Parliament Secretariat. Foreign nationals have to apply through their embassies or high commissions. Visitors can enter the public galleries of the Indian Parliament with prior permission, after receiving an official pass. To enter the library, an entry pass can be obtained from the Visitor's reception on Raisina Road by providing a letter of introduction from a Member of Parliament.

The Parliament House or Sansad Bhavan is the seat of the two houses of the Indian Legislature- the Lok Sabha and the Rajya Sabha and is therefore by default the most important administrative building in the country and of course in New Delhi. This circular building well known for its colonnade was built as a part of the New Delhi project undertaken by the British Government for its new capital.

The parliament building was designed by Herbert Baker, who along with Edwin Lutyens was responsible for the architecture of the much of New Delhi, notably the state administrative buildings along Rajpath. The architecture of the Parliament house actually invoked much criticism among connoisseurs. An article by Robert Byron in Architectural Review, January 1931describes it thus: "The Council Chamber has been Sir Herbert's unhappiest venture. Its effect from a distance has been described. It resembles a Spanish bull-ring, lying like a mill-wheel dropped accidentally on its side." However, this apparently faultily designed building that passes for the Indian Parliament House, is quite a feast for the layman's eyes.

Architecture of Parliament House

The Parliament House is a huge circular, colonnaded building of sandstone located to the northwest of Vijay Chowk. The building comprises of three semicircular chambers for the Lok Sabha, Rajya Sabha and a Central Library crowned by a 29.9m high dome over which now flaps the tri colors of the Indian flag. The three semi-circular chambers were originally designed for the Chamber of Princes, the Council of State and the Legislative Assembly. The building has a diameter of 170.69m and covers 2.02 hectares in area, with colonnaded verandahs lined with 144 identical columns each 8.23 m high enclosing the entire circumference.

The Central Hall, located at the centre of the circular Parliament House, is surrounded by three Chambers and three well laid-out courtyards with lush green lawns and fountains. Short passages radiating from three equidistant points on the circumference of the Hall connect the Lok Sabha Chamber, the Rajya Sabha Chamber and the earlier Library Hall. The entire Parliament

House Estate is enclosed by an ornamental red sand stone wall with iron gates.

Entry and photography inside the Parliament is free but prior to permission from relevant authorities.

Fast - Facts:

Introduction

The Parliament House or Sansad Bhavan is the seat of the two houses of the Indian Legislature- the Lok Sabha and the Rajya Sabha and is therefore by default the most important administrative building in the country and of course in New Delhi. This circular building well known for its colonnade was built as a part of the New Delhi project undertaken by the British Government for its new capital. The parliament building was designed by Herbert Baker, who along with Edwin Lutyens was responsible for the architecture of the much of New Delhi, notably the state administrative buildings along Rajpath. Below is a list of Fast Facts on Parliament House for a smooth and convenient tour of the most important building in India.

Fast Facts on Parliament House

The Parliament House is located on the northwest of Vijay Chowk, next to the Secretariat buildings at the end of Parliament Street (Sansad Marg). Also Known as- Sansad Bhavan.

Entry-

Entry is free but subject to prior permission. One can visit the parliament irrespective of whether the houses are in session, with an official pass.

Permit-

Foreigners/Citizens: from their embassies or High commissions/ from the reception office on Raisina Road.

Mode of Transport -

Public buses, auto-richshaws, taxis or metro rail can be availed to reach North and South Block. Each of these, are easily and frequently available.

Nearest terminals-

The nearest rail station is New Delhi station, the nearest metro station is Central Secretariat and the nearest airport is Indira Gandhi International Airport.

Nearest City Centre-

Connaught Place, the heart of New Delhi is very near and is the hub of the best eateries, shops and markets.

Delhi Zoo

The National Zoological Park of Delhi is popularly known as Delhi Zoo. Adjacent to the Purana Qila, Delhi Zoo is located on the southern side of the fort. Although it is an artificial habitat, the animals here are provided with spacious enclosures and other arrangements necessary for their survival in a man-made environment. Spread over an area of 240 acres, it is one of the better laid out zoological parks of the country,

The zoo features quite an amazing range of flora and fauna. Over one thousand varieties of mammals, reptiles and avian species can be seen here. Leopard cat, Indian Rhinoceros, Hippopotamus, Black Buck, Indian Gazelle and Lion-tailed macaque are some of the commonly found animals here. It also has nearly all varieties of deer spotted in the country. Don't miss the white tiger from Rewa, the elephant which plays a harmonica and the leopards. The zoo is home to many species now endangered in India. Several species of migratory birds have made this spot their favorite haunting ground. Winter is the time when the winged visitors including, storks, ducks and other species throng the large lake at the entrance of Delhi zoo.

Although battery operated vehicles are available for nominal charges which will take you on a tour around the park, but, you get the best deal when you are on foot. There are arrow signs placed in the park to guide you the direction. There is also a canteen where you can have good food because no eatables are allowed inside the park except drinking water. Although, there are many drinking water counters at various places in the park for convenient of the visitors.

The early hours of opening or late afternoon before the closing are the better times of the day to visit the zoo. Winter undoubtedly is the best season. Hot summer months should be avoided as animals prefer to rest in their hideouts and are not easily seen.

Fast - Facts:

Here are some facts about the Delhi Zoo which would help you to have a quick glance of this popular park in Delhi. Also, this will make it a lot more convenient for you.

Location
Adjacent to the Purana Qila, Delhi Zoo is located on the southern side of the fort.

Built In

The zoo was built in 1957.

Special Feature

The zoo has a library which is a storehouse of information on birds, animals, plants and common species of birds and animals in India.

How to Reach

Delhi Zoo being located in the capital city, can be reached from any corner of the country.

<u>Nearest International Airport</u>: Indira Gandhi International Airport
<u>Nearest Railway Station</u>: Nizamuddin Railway Station
<u>Nearest Metro Station</u>: Central Secretariat
<u>Nearest Bus Stop</u>: Local buses from various points
<u>Best Time To Visit</u>: Winter undoubtedly is the best season to visit Delhi Zoo.

Nearby Attractions:

The places nearby the Delhi Zoo are some of the most popular tourist spots in Delhi. If you are planning for a visit to this popular park, keep some time for a trip to these unique sites. Rich in historical and cultural significance, these places are a must-see.

Nearby Attractions of Delhi Zoo are Nila Gumbad, Purana Qila, Humayun's Tomb, Sabz Burz, Nili Chhatri, India Gate, Ashokan Rock Edict, Nizam-ud-din's Shrine and Khairul Manzil Masjid.

Nila Gumbad

Located near the Delhi Zoo, Nila Gumbad can be best described as Humayun's architectural legacy.

Purana Qila

Purana Qila is located on the bank of the Yamuna River. A good example of medieval military architecture, the ramparts of the Qila cover a perimeter of nearly 2 kilometers. The imposing walls of the Qila are 18 meters in height.

Humayun's Tomb

Humayun's senior widow Bega Begum built this magnificent tomb in Delhi in 1565. With high arches and a full double dome, it is one of the most beautiful Mughal monuments.

Sabz Burz

Sabz Burz is one of the many structures which bear Humayun's architectural legacy.

Nili Chhatri

This Hindu temple in the Yamuna bazar is dedicated to Lord Shiva. Legend has it that the eldest Pandava brother, Yudhisthira established the temple and the Nigambodh Ghat adjacent to it.

India Gate

This 42 mt. high stone-arch of victory was built in 1931 and was designed by Sir Edwin Lutyens. It stands at the eastern end of Rajpath. It was previously known as the All India War Memorial.

Ashokan Rock Edict

The centuries old Ashokan Rock Edict was discovered in 1966. It is testimony to the fact that Delhi was an important area even during the time of the Mauryan Emperor Ashoka.

Nizam-ud-din's Shrine

It is the shrine of the famous Muslim Sufi and mystic saint, Sheikh Hazrat Nizamuddin Aulia Chishti. It is located about 2 km. from Humayun's tomb.

Khairul Manzil Masjid

This 16th c mosque is located opposite the Purana Qila and the Delhi Zoo entrance. It was built in 1561 by Maham Anga, the most influential wet nurse of the Mughal Emperor Akbar. It is considered as one of 'the most auspicious of houses'. This is not all. The places near the Delhi Zoo have some of the finest places to eat and shop.

Sweet Corner, Nathu's in Sunder Nagar Market, Hotel Oberoi, Flavors of Defence colony, Indian Habitat Center in Lodi Road, Karims at Nizamuddin and legions of roadside food stalls will give a taste of a lip smacking variety of cuisines. Of course, the dishes typical to Delhi are not to be missed.

Sunder Nagar Market for antiques, jewelry, brassware, Connaught Place for jewelry, books, art galleries, leather goods and clothes, Central Cottage Industries Emporia for merchandise and curios, Janpath for clothes and low priced gifts, souvenirs and curios and Palika Bazaar for electronic items are famous shopping spots near the Delhi Zoo.

Railway Museum

The railway museum in New Delhi is a national museum of its kind situated in the heart of the capital city of India. The Railway Museum or the National Railway Museum of India was established in 1977 about 30 years ago. This Railway Museum showcases old models of Railway engines and the relevant locomotives, old railway models and much more which is worth a visit. National Railway Museum also helps to form an idea about the functioning of Indian railway 30 years ago.

What to see:

It tells you about the mechanisms used to run trains which were essentially not driven by electricity at that time. Railway Museum New Delhi has a wide and assorted collection of atypical and antique steam locomotives, carriages, saloons and other railway relics. The museum premise houses both live exhibits as well as working/non-working models in its indoor gallery. The museum runs a toy train around its grounds on regular days except the holidays. On some special days or on an occasion the Old Patiala State Steam Monorail is steamed up and runs on its track around the museum to entertain the guests and tourists.

National railway Museum Delhi is a small arena consisting of railway memorabilia. The museum artifacts also include the skull of an elephant killed when it collided with a mail train in Bengal, in 1894. The last steam engine whereas the first electric-powered engine of the1930s are kept on display. One of the most interesting features are the special carriages belonging to British and Indian lords, namely the Viceregal dining car, the

Maharaja of Mysore's personal train with both sleeping and day compartments and the Gaekwar of Baroda's Saloon.

There are many other things to know about the Railway Museum Delhi:

- Railway Museum – Fast Facts
- Annual Events
- Nearby Attractions

Rajghat in Delhi

Rajghat in Delhi is the cremation site of Gandhiji, Mohandas Karamchand Gandhi who is most reveredly remembered as the Father of Nation. This memorial is located between the main Ring Road which is now known as the Mahatma Gandhi Road and the banks of the Yamuna River, just southeast of Red Fort. Set amidst deep green lawns and fountains, Rajghat is surrounded by a lovely wooded area and several exotic trees creating a serene ambience.

The mortal remains of Mahatma Gandhi were cremated at this ghat or stepped embankment at the edge of the Yamuna river on 31st January in following his assassination while walking to his customary prayer meeting at Birla House.

The structure of the Samadhi reflects simplicity. The brick platform on which his body had been burned, a black marble platform of some twelve feet by twelve feet square and two feet deep and a surrounding while marble fence were erected and the shores were landscaped. The last words of Mahatma Gandhi, 'Hey Ram' are inscribed on the memorial platform which is flanked by an eternal flame.

Earthworks around the cenotaph protect it from the flooding Yamuna. Inside this enclosure trees were planted with and little square plots of white pebble stones added for decoration.

There are trees labeled near the platform planted by visiting dignitaries such as Queen Elizabeth II, Ho Chi Minh, the former Australian Prime Minister Gough Whitman and the former US president Dwight Eisenhower.

People of every class visit the memorial to pay their homage to Mahatma whom they fondly call the 'Bapu'. Good parking facilities are available and all basic facilities for visitors are present within the premises.

Life of Mahatma Gandhi

Life of Mahatma Gandhi, the most respected political and spiritual leaders of the 1900's, has always been part of history-book stuff. Mohandas Karamchand Gandhi was born on October 2, 1869 in Porbandar, India. He got married to Kasturba at the early age of 13. He studied law in London and returned to India in 1891 to practice. In 1893 he took on a one-year contract for legal work in South Africa.

It was through witnessing the racism, prejudice and injustice against himself and other Indians in South Africa that Gandhi started to fight for his people's status and his own place in society. Gandhi stayed in South Africa for 21 years working to secure rights for Indian people. He employed a method of action called Satyagraha based upon the principles of courage, nonviolence and truth. He promoted nonviolence and civil disobedience as the most appropriate methods for obtaining political and social goals. In 1915 Gandhi returned to India at the end of his contract.

In May 1915, Gandhi founded an ashram on the outskirts of Ahmedabad and called it Satyagrah Ashram which is also known as the Sabarmati Ashram. There lodged twenty five men and women who took vows of truth, celibacy, ahimsa, non-possession, control of the palate and service of the Indian people. Gandhi's first major achievements came in 1918 when he started the Champaran agitation and the Kheda Satyagraha.

Using the principles of Satyagraha he led the campaign for Indian independence from the British Government. Gandhi was arrested several times by the British for his political activities. He taught the Indians the need of unity among the different religions, languages and classes of society and used several fasts in order to advocate the principle of non-violence. It was the Rowlatt Bill with its denial of civil liberties which finally brought Gandhi into active Indian politics. From 1919 to his death in 1948, he occupied the centre of the Indian political arena and changed the entire character of the political scene in India.

On August 15, 1947, India was partitioned and became independent. Gandhi refused to attend the celebrations in the capital and went to Calcutta where communal riots were still raging. On January 13, 1948, at the age of 78, he began a fast with the purpose of stopping the bloodshed. After 5 days, the opposing leaders promised to stop the fighting and Gandhi broke his fast. Twelve days later, a Hindu fanatic, Nathuram Godse assassinated him.

Fast - Facts:

Here are some facts about the Rajghat which would help you to have a quick glance of this famous memorial in Delhi. Also, this will make it a lot more convenient for you.

Location

This memorial is located between the main Ring Road which is now known as the Mahatma Gandhi Road and the banks of the Yamuna River, just southeast of Red Fort.

Special Feature

A prayer service is arranged for on every Friday, the day he was assassinated, at 5.30 pm in the evening.

How to Reach

Rajghat being located in the capital city, can be reached from any corner of the country.

Nearest International Airport: Indira Gandhi International Airport
Nearest Railway Station: Old Delhi Railway Station
Nearest Metro Station: Kashmiri Gate
Nearest Bus Stop: Local buses from various points

Nearby Attractions

The places nearby the Rajghat are some of the most popular tourist spots in Delhi. If you are planning for a visit to this famous memorial, keep some time for a trip to these unique sites. Rich in historical and cultural significance, these places are a must-see.

Nearby Attractions of Rajghat in Delhi are Vijay Ghat, Vir Bhumi, Shakti Sthal, Shanti Van, National Gandhi Museum, Zinat-ul-masjid, Feroz Shah Kotla and Khuni Darwaza.

Vijay Ghat

Just near the small artificial lake, to the extreme north of landscaped gardens of Rajghat, is Vijay Ghat, where India's second Prime Minister Lal Bahadur Shastri was cremated in 1966.

Vir Bhumi

Located next to Rajghat is the memorial of the youngest prime minister of India, Rajiv Gandhi. Rajiv Gandhi was the first son of Indira Gandhi. He was appointed as prime minister within hours of his mother's assassination in 1984. He was assassinated by an LTTE suicide bomber, at Sriperumbudur in Tamil Nadu, in 1991.

Shakti Sthal

Located to the north of Vir Bhumi, Shakti Sthal is the memorial of India's first and only lady Prime Minister, Indira Gandhi. She was the only child of Jawahar Lal Nehru, India's first prime minister.

Shanti Van

It is the memorial of India's great leader and first prime minister, Jawahar Lal Nehru. It is located to the north of Shakti Sthal and Rajghat. Jawahar Lal Nehru is considered as the father of institutional democracy of the country.

National Gandhi Museum

This two storey museum is located just opposite the Rajghat. It has a very rich collection of photographs, relics, memorabilia associated with Mahatma Gandhi and also books, journals and documents, audio-visual materials, exhibitions and art pieces.

Zinat-ul-masjid

It is also known as 'Ghata Masjid'. Built in 1707 AD by Zinat-ul-Nissa Begum, the daughter of Emperor Aurangzeb, the mosque is believed to be a replica of the magnificent Jama Masjid on a smaller scale.

Feroz Shah Kotla

Located near the famous Feroz Shah Kotla Cricket Stadium, it was the majestic citadel of Ferozabad, the Fifth city of Delhi. The great builder and Emperor Firoz Shah Tughlaq built the city of Ferozabad with its citadel in 1354.

Khuni Darwaza

Khuni Darwaza or Bloody Gate was built by Emperor Sher Shah Suri in 16th century, as one of the gates of his city Shergarh. This double storied majestic gate got its name after the first war of Indian Independence in 1857 when a British officer killed the remaining descendants of the last Mughal emperor Bahadur Shah Zafar. The bodies were displayed for public viewing before taken to Kotwali.

This is not all. The places near Rajghat have some of the finest places to eat and shop. Hotel Inter-Continental in Connaught Place, Karim Hotel, Ghantewala sweet shop, food stalls near Jama Masjid, Paranthewali gali, Natraj hotel, Chor Bizarre of Broadway Hotel, Daryaganj's Flora, Peshwari, Moti Mahal Restaurant, Worker's canteen of Inter-State Bus terminal and legions of roadside food stalls will give a taste of a lip smacking variety of cuisines. Of course, the dishes typical to Delhi are not to be missed.

Chandni Chowk for curios, souvenirs, silver and glass bead jewelry, Nai Sarak for books, Chor bazaar for electronic goods, Daryaganj book market on Sunday and Chatta Chowk in Red Fort for traditional and contemporary jewelry and handicrafts are famous shopping spots near the Rajghat.

Rashtrapati Bhavan

Apart from being the capital of India, Delhi is a fascinating city with pleasant contradictions. Comprising of Old Delhi and New Delhi, the city is home to famous tourist destinations like the Laxmi Narayan Temple, India Gate, Jama Masjid, Red Fort, Qutub Minar, Humayun's Tomb, and the vivacious shopping bazaar of Chandni Chowk. One such tourist attraction in Delhi is the Rashtrapati Bhavan, the official residence of the President of India.

Background

The Palace of Rashtrapati Bhavan is located in New Delhi. Until 1950 it was known as Viceroy's House and served as the residence of the Governor-General of India. On 12th December 1911, during the Delhi Durbar year it was announced by King George that the capital of India would be shifted from Calcutta to Delhi. As the plan for New Delhi took shape, the Governor-General's residence was given an enormous scale and prominent position. The British architect Edwin Landseer Lutyens, a key member of the city-planning process, was handed the prime architectural responsibility to design the building. The palace, comprising of more than 350 Rooms, was constructed to affirm the permanence of British rule in India.

After Indian independence in 1947, the now ceremonial governor-general continued to live there, being succeeded by the Indian President in 1950 when India became a republic and the house was renamed Rashtrapati Bhavan.

Description

The elaborate dome-like structure on top of the Rashtrapati Bhavan is known as Chuttri. Various Indian designs were added to the building including several circular stone basins on the top of the palace. There was also a traditional Indian chujja or chhajja, which took the place of a frieze in classical architecture. There were also statues of elephants and fountain sculptures of cobras in the gardens, as well as grilles made from red sandstone called jaalis.

The front of the palace, on the east side, has twelve unevenly spaced columns with the Delhi order capitals. These capitals have a fusion of acanthus leaves with the four pendant Indian bells that are part of the Hindu and Buddhist religions. In the North Block, there are separate wings for the Viceroy, and another wing for guests. At the centre of the main part of the palace is Durbar's Hall underneath the main dome.

Entrance

Visitors require special permission from Government of India Tourist Office to enter Rastrapathi Bhavan. The Mughal garden, displaying numerous types of roses, remains open to the public only in the month of February when the flowers gloriously bloom.

How to reach

The nearest airport is the Indira Gandhi International Airport located 23 km southwest of Central Delhi and the domestic terminal at Palam is 5 km away from the international terminal. Taxi and coach transfer is available from both International and Domestic Arrivals.

Architecture of Rashtrapati Bhavan:

Perhaps the most dominant symbol of the largest democracy in the world as well as a poignant statement of her sovereignty, the Rashtrapati Bhavan is perhaps the greatest pride of India. Thus, it is hardly surprisingly that the architecture of the Rashtrapati Bhavan too is one that enhances the rich history of Indian artistic and architectural endeavors.

Designed by Edwin Landseer Lutyens, the Rashtrapati Bhavan was originally built as the residence of the British viceroy of India after the capital of the then British ruled India was transferred from Calcutta to Delhi. Besides Lutyens, the construction was designed by a number of other architects including Chief Engineer Hugh Keeling there were many Indian contractors.

Comprising of four floors and 340 rooms, the Rashtrapati Bhavan is constructed over an area of 200,000 square feet incurring a cost of construction that along with that of the Mughal Gardens reached up to 14 million rupees. The most prominent feature of the architecture of the Rashtrapati Bhavan is the dome that forms one of the most prestigious sights of the capital city of New Delhi. A blend of the architectural patterns of Rome as well as the Sanchi Stupa of India, the Rashtrapati Bhavan is a harmonious representation of a number of different architectural styles of both Europe as well as India.

Fast - Facts:

Location

The Rashtrapati Bhavan built on the Raisina Hill is located on the western end of the Rajpath just about a mile away from Connaught Place.

Built by

Built as the official residence of the Viceroy of India after the capital of British ruled India was changed from Calcutta to Delhi, the Rashtrapati Bhavan was designed by Sir Edwin Lutyens.

Admission charges

Though there are no admission fees at the Rashtrapati Bhavan yet it is important that prior permission is taken before visiting the site. Prior permission is also required for photography at the site.

How To Reach:

Located in the heart of the city of Delhi, reaching Rashtrapati Bhavan can be easily accomplished as it is well-connected by:

<u>Nearest airport</u> - Indira Gandhi International Airport
<u>Nearest railway station</u> - New Delhi Railway Station
<u>Nearest metro station</u> - Central Secretariat

Must-see:

An important added attraction of the Rashtrapati Bhavan is the "change of guards" ceremony that takes place on the premises of the Rashtrapati Bhavan every Saturday.

Safdarjung's Tomb

Apart from being the capital of India, Delhi is a fascinating city with pleasant contradictions. Comprising of Old Delhi and New Delhi, the city is home to famous tourist destinations like the Laxmi Narayan Temple, India Gate, Jama Masjid, Red Fort, Qutub Minar, Humayun's Tomb, and the vivacious shopping bazaar of Chandni Chowk. One such tourist attraction in Delhi is the Safdarjung's Tomb, the last of the mausoleums of the Mughal dynasty.

Background

Safdarjung's Tomb was built by Nawab Shuja-ud-Daula in 1753-54 AD for his father, Mirza Mukin Abul Mansur Khan 'Safdarjung'. Mirza Mukin Abul Mansur Khan was the wazir of emperor Ahmed Shah and Safdarjang was a title, either awarded to him by the king, or he assumed himself. Erected roughly on the pattern of Humayun's tomb, Safdarjung's tomb is set in the middle of a garden, which spreads over an area of 300 sq m. This garden is laid down on the pattern of the Mughal Charbagh style.

Description

The tomb was built by an Ethiopian architect, Bilal Mohammed Khan, at an exorbitant cost of Rs 3 lakhs. The marble and sandstone facing used for it was abstracted from the tomb of

Abdul Rahim Khan-i-Khanan. The tomb is made of buff-colored sandstone with the intermittent use of red sandstone and marble. There are two graves here, one of Safdarjung and the other apparently that of his wife's.

The central chamber is carved and finely polished, surrounded by rhombic and square compartments. Sunlight enters through the latticework. Constructed of small hard-baked lakori bricks, the central structure has double-storey minarets at the corners and a globular marble dome, and is surrounded by eight rooms. The three-domed and arched mosque with whaleback roofing at the entrance was added later.

There are beautiful pavilions on either side of the Safdarjung Tomb, known as Moti Mahal or the pearl palace, Jangli Mahal or the sylvan palace and Badshah Pasand or the emperor's favorite.

How to reach

Safdarjung Tomb lies at the Lodi road, New Delhi. To reach there, the nearest airport is the Indira Gandhi International Airport located 23 km southwest of Central Delhi and the domestic terminal at Palam is 5 km away from the international terminal. Taxi and coach transfer is available from both International and Domestic Arrivals.

Architecture of Safdarjung's Tomb

The Architecture of Safdarjung's Tomb in Delhi stands as the last flickering specimen of Mughal creations. One of the final Mughal constructions, this mausoleum for ages has been a witness to the changing times and bygone dynasties.

Safdurjang was the Wazir of the Mughal Empire who was also honored as the Governor of Oudh. After his demise in 1754, the Safdarjung's Tomb was constructed by his son Shujauddaulah.

The Safdarjung's Tomb reflects the striking features of the Mughal mausoleums with its arched gateways, octagonal towers and sprawling gardens.

The architecture of Safdarjung's Tomb is quite similar to the Humayun's Tomb. The mausoleum has pavilions known as the Badshah Pasand and Jangli Mahal. Sprawling acres of greenery surround the tomb which is about 300metres in area.

The Safdarjung's Tomb is covered by a bulbous dome and has four polygonal towers inlaid with marble work. The tomb is built of red sandstone and it also represents the features of Mughal architecture.

The central chamber of the tomb has eight compartments. The edifice is placed on a high platform.

Considered to be one of the major tourist attractions, the Safdarjung's tomb is a famous historical monument that reminds of the bygone Mughal dynasty and the monarchs who once ruled Delhi.

Fast - Facts:

Location:

located near the crossing of Safdarjung Road and Aurobindo Marg near Safdarjung Airport in New Delhi.

History:

Built by Nawab Shujauddaulah in the memory of his father, it was constructed in the year 1753-54. Safdarjung was the Governor of Oudh.

Architecture:

Considered to be the final specimen of Mughal and Islamic architecture, the Safdarjung's Tomb is a replica of Humayun's Tomb. The arched gateways, sandstone construction and reflection pools indicate that they are the typical features of Mughal mausoleums. There are beautiful pavilions in the tomb which are the Badshah Pasand, Moti Mahal and the Jangli Mahal.

How to Reach:

Just a 20 minutes drive from the Connaught Place, the Safdarjung's Tomb is easily accessible and tourists can take taxis, auto rickshaws or the metro rail.

Attractions:

There is an interesting library in the gateway which will make you aware about the history of the place as well as about the monuments and history of Delhi.

Charges for Photography: INR 25

Nearest Shopping Venues:

- Jorbagh Market: It is famous for art and crafts, designer wear
- Khan Market: Known for curios, artifacts and books
- Sarojini Nagar Market: Famous for the clothes and household goods

Nearest Metro Station: Central Secretariat

Nearest Airport: Indira Gandhi International Airport

Nearest Railway Station: Nizammuddin Station

Nearby Attractions:

Tourists visiting Safdarjang's Tomb also should visit the nearby attractions of Safdarjang's Tomb. The monument Safdarjang's Tomb located in the Lodi Road in Delhi is one of the 18th century Mughal Monuments which is built in the memory of Shujauddaulah's father Safdarjang. Safdarjang was the governor of Oudh and the tomb built in his memory is the last flickering specimen of Mughal and Islamic architecture.

Tourists visiting the Safdarjang's Tomb will find the arched gateways, reflection pools, sandstone construction and marble work which are the typical features of Mughal creations.

Tourist Places near Safdarjang's Tomb:

Dilli Haat:

If you wish to take a glimpse on the kaleidoscopic fabric of India then visit the Dilli Haat. One of the nearby attractions of Safdurjung's Tomb, it draws tourists and specially the art and craft lovers from all over India. This crafts village of Delhi spreading over six acres of area is the confluence point of different arts and handicrafts of India. Different states, different colors and different flavors, Dilli Haat is a fusion of these differences.

India Gate:

A fascinating and wonderful monument built in the commemoration of Indian soldiers is located near the Safdarjang's Tomb. It is also considered to be one of the nearby attractions of Safdurjung's Tomb.

Lodi Gardens:

Built by the Lodis, these serene and beautiful gardens with the remnants of historical relics is one of the favorite tourist attractions of Delhi. Indulge yourself the cool shades of acres of greenery or get nos talgic about the bygone dynasties in the beautiful environs of the Lodi Gardens.

Nearby Shopping Venues:

The nearby shopping venues which are located beside Safdarjang's Tomb are:

- Jorbagh Market: Famous for art and crafts, designer wear
- Khan Market: Famous for curios, artifacts and books
- Sarojini Nagar Market: Famous for clothes and household goods

Jama Masjid

Facing west, the Jama Masjid is covered on three sides with open arched colonnades with a tower like gateway in the center. Also called Masjid-I-Jahanuma or the 'mosque commanding view of the world', the Jama Masjid is a constructional wonder with alternating strips of red sandstone and marble.

The mosque owes much of the respect associated with it to the relics of Mohammad, which it houses. These include Quran written on deerskin, a red beard-hair of the prophet, his sandals and his footprint, embedded in a marble slab, all of which are still preserved.

Architecturally, the Jama Masjid is similar to many other mosques that the Emperor of Architecture, Shah Jahan built all around his realm. These include mosques by the same name in cities like Ajmer, Agra and a number of others. The courtyard of the Jama Masjid, which is completely built of red sandstone, is accessible from the east, north and south by three different flights of stairs. These steps are used to house markets, entertainers as well as food stalls. The mosque also housed a Madrassah near the southern side of the mosque which had been pulled down after the Sepoy Mutiny of 1857.

India is known for her unity in diversity. People belonging to different faiths and different mental thoughts co-exist in the country with perfect harmony within themselves, contributing thereby to the strength of the Indian fabric in general. Their places of worship too, are thus sacred not just to themselves but to their fellow-countrymen as well, irrespective of the faith they follow. One of these is the Jama Masjid in Delhi, built by the Mughal emperor Shah Jahan in 1656. Generally considered to be the largest and most respected mosque in India, the Jama Masjid is one of the most famous landmarks of the country, symbolizing for the country's Muslim population a guide to the religious doctrines.

History:

Showcasing India's fine blend of religions, the Jama Masjid is one of the greatest examples of the fine fabric of secularism that envelopes the entirety of India. The mosque which is part of the historic complex of the Red Fort in Delhi draws countless of visitors each day, many of whom are drawn to this revered site by the history of the Jama Masjid.

The mosque was built by Shahjahan inside his fort city of Shahjahanabad or the Red Fort as it is known today. Planned and designed by the brilliant Mughal architect Ostad Khalil, the mosque was built at a cost that was around 10 crores, a colossal figure in the medieval era, even considering the grandeur of the enterprise. The mosque was begun in 1650 which saw over 5,000 workers involved in the labor which was to see the largest mosque in India completed six years after its foundation stone was laid.

The mosque in the medieval period had certain areas restricted for the use of the emperor and the other members of the royal family. These included the largest and the highest gate of the complex located on the eastern side of the Jama Masjid.

Besides its obvious religious significance, the mosque was also used for housing a Madrassah near its southern side, which was pulled down after the Sepoy Mutiny of 1857.

Much of the respect that is accorded to the Jama Masjid is due to the fact that the mosque is famous for housing some of the notable relics of Prophet Mohammad, which includes, the Quran written on deerskin, a red beard-hair of the prophet, his sandals and his footprint, embedded in a marble slab, all of which are still preserved

Annual Events:

The Jama Masjid symbolizes to most Indians an amalgamation of religion and history where each strives to bring in a sense of unity not just amongst the Muslims but also amongst their non-Islamic brethren. The mosque which was built by Shah Jahan was originally constructed as part of the Mughal emperor's newly constructed capital of Shahjahanabad or the Red Fort as it is known as today. At that period, the mosque had special chambers that were dedicated to the prayer sessions of the emperor and the other members of the royal family. The importance that the Jama Masjid enjoyed during the period, has, however, not diminished today and is still strongly held on to just like the other traditions and customs that are still associated with the various annual events of the Jama Masjid.

One of the most important features of the mosque is that the chief cleric of the mosque has always been till now the direct descendant of the chief cleric who was invited by Shah Jahan to come to Delhi from Bukhara at the time of the inauguration of the Jama Masjid in 1635. It is perhaps this authenticity that makes the Chief Cleric of the Jama Masjid one of the most respected figures amongst India's Islamic brethren. Thus, the celebration of important Islamic festivals finds their greatest expressions on the premises of the Jama Masjid. These include the important Muslim festivals like Id-ul-Fitr and Id-ul-Zoha when thousands of followers of Islam throng the premises of the Jama Masjid to offer their prayers on its auspicious grounds.

Fast - Facts:

Location

Located on Netaji Subhash Marg, Old Delhi, the Jama Masjid is at a distance of just around 500 meters west of the Red Fort is located close to a number of other tourist attractions of Delhi.

Built by

Built by the emperor of architecture, Shahjahan inside his newly built capital Shahjahanabad, the Jama Masjid was built in 1656.

Nature & Architectural style

Showcasing a rich influence of Persian architecture, the Jama Masjid is one of the oldest mosques of India.

Timings

The summer timings at the Jama Masjid are 7 a.m. to 12.15 p.m and again from 1.45 p.m. to till sunset. The winter timings are from 8.30 am-12.15 pm & again from 1.45 pm till sunset.

Admission charges

Though the entrance to the mosque is not charged and can be accessed at any time except during the time of prayers by people of all religions, photography is charged at a rate of 1.N.R. 20 for Indian visitors and I.N.R. 150 for foreigners.

How to Reach:

Located in the heart of the city of Old Delhi, reaching the Jama Masjid can be easily accomplished as it is well-connected by:

<u>Nearest airport</u> - Indira Gandhi International Airport
<u>Nearest railway station</u> - Old Delhi Railway Station
Nearest metro station - Kashmir Gate

Nearby Attractions:

One of the most respected places of religious worship in the entirety of the country as well as the oldest mosque in India, the Jama Masjid is one of the leading tourist attractions of Delhi, popular not just amongst the followers of Islam but also believers of other religions. The mosque, which is located inside the complex of the Red Fort or Shahjahanabad as it was known as before, has a number of nearby attractions to offer the visitors to the site in addition to its own pristine beauty.

Nearby Attractions:

Red Fort

One of the most important symbols of India's sovereign democracy, the Red Fort was once the capital of the Mughal dynasty after it was built by Shahjahan as his capital called Shahjahanabad. A huge complex showcasing life as it was in during the Golden Rule of the Mughals, the Red Fort is a must-visit while on a trip to Delhi.

Qutub Minar

Another important symbol of the historic city of Delhi, the Qutub Minar is an iron tower built in 1199 by Qutubuddin Aibak, which has till today, not shown a single speck of rust.

Chandni Chowk

One of the important bazaars of Shahjahan's Red Fort, this historic bazaar is today, one of the oldest trading centers in northern India, showcasing some of India's finest examples in terms of jewelry, fabrics, handicrafts as well as an array of mouthwatering roadside snacks.

India Gate

Built as a memorial for the Indian soldiers who were killed in the 1st World War, the India Gate is an imposing structure that arches to give a glimpse of the red sandstone structure of the Red Fort.

Lakshmi Narayan Temple

Located in the heart of the city of New Delhi, the Lakshmi Narayan Temple is one of the major tourist attractions of the city. Enchantingly carved depicting some of the finest gems of Hindu theology, the Lakshmi Narayan Temple was built in 1938 by Raja Baldev Das and is situated on the western portion of Connaught Place, one of the most important areas of the city of New Delhi.

History

Renowned as Birla Mandir, the Lakshmi Narayan temple was constructed in 1938 by the industrialist BD Birla. Located in the heart of the city on Mandir Marg, west of Connaught Place, the temple is dedicated to the Hindu deities Lakshmi (the Goddess of wealth and prosperity) and Narayana (the Preserver). Other idols present in the temple are that of Lord Shiva and Goddess Durga.

The temple elaborately celebrates the festival of Janmashthami and has a special display which attracts hordes of devotees on the occasion. Beautiful gardens and an exotic pool adorn the temple, with the architecture resembling that of the Hindu temples built in the Orissan style. The highest tower in the temple is of 165ft, while the auxiliary towers reach 116ft. The walls of the temple are decorated with various Hindu symbols and quotes from the Gita and the Upanishads. There is also a temple dedicated to Lord Buddha designed with fresco paintings describing his life and work. The rear of the temple has been developed as artificial mountainous scenery with fountains and waterfalls.

Inaugurated by the Father of the Nation, Mahatma Gandhi, the temple is unique for being open to all castes. A symbolic structure at the entrance welcomes people of all faiths and classes.

Architecture

Built in the style of Orissa, the temple portrays a rich influence of the north-Indian styles of architecture as well. The entire complex is adorned with frescos and paintings depicting scenes and narrating stories from the major texts of Hinduism. Besides this, just behind the temple is an artificial landscape with fountains and waterfalls.

Religious Basis

The presiding deity of the temple is Lord Vishnu, Hinduism's emblem of wealth and prosperity. However, the temple is also home to a number of other shrines dedicated to deities like Lord Shiva, Lord Ganesha and Hanuman. The Vedic texts are also enshrined in the temple which also houses a Buddha temple inside its premises. In the northern portion of the temple lies the Geeta Bhavan, dedicated to Lord Krishna.

Annual Events:

Renowned as Birla Mandir, the Lakshmi Narayan temple was constructed in 1938 by the industrialist BD Birla. Located in the heart of the city on Mandir Marg, west of Connaught Place, the temple is dedicated to the Hindu deities Lakshmi (the Goddess of wealth and prosperity) and Narayana (the Preserver). Following are the special annual events that take place at Lakshmi Narayan Temple -

Ram Navami

During the Hindu festival of Ram Navami, which falls during the month of April, devotees throng in large numbers at the temple. This festival is a celebration of the birth of Lord Rama, an incarnation of Lord Vishnu. Several local theatres enact the epic of Ramayana during this festival.

Janmashthami

The temple is known for elaborately celebrating the festival of Janmashthami, commemorating the birth of Lord Krishna, and has a special display which attracts hordes of devotees on the occasion. During Janmashthami, the temple is lit up and thousands of devotees come here to pay reverence to the deity and celebrate the occasion.

Fast - facts:

Renowned as Birla Mandir, the Lakshmi Narayan temple was constructed in 1938 by the industrialist BD Birla. The temple is dedicated to the Hindu deities Lakshmi (the Goddess of wealth and prosperity) and Narayana (the Preserver). Following are some fast facts about Lakshmi Narayan Temple -

Location

In the heart of the city on Mandir Marg, west of Connaught Place in Central Delhi.

Time to Visit

Open on all days of the year, round the clock, but preferably be there during aarti in the morning or evening. There is no admission fee, as it is open to all. It requires approximately half an hour looking around this magnificent construction.

How to Reach

To reach the Lakshmi Narayan Temple, you can fly down to the Indira Gandhi International Airport in Delhi. You can either avail of local buses from various points within the city to reach the monument, or hire auto-rickshaws and taxis or take the metro rail. The nearest functional Metro station is Central Secretariat, while the nearest railway station is the New Delhi Railway Station.

Nearby Places to Eat

Some of the popular eat-outs near Lakshmi Narayan Temple are Hotel Le Meridien, Imperial Hotel, Hotel Inter-Continental, Parikrama Revolving restaurant, Gaylord, El Rodeo, Bercos, Zen restaurant, Delhi Darbar, Nizam's and Standard Restaurant.

Nearby Attractions:

Renowned as Birla Mandir, the Lakshmi Narayan temple was constructed in 1938 by the industrialist BD Birla. Located in the heart of the city on Mandir Marg, west of Connaught Place, the temple is dedicated to the Hindu deities Lakshmi (the Goddess of wealth and prosperity) and Narayana (the Preserver). Following are some of the tourist attractions near Lakshmi Narayan Temple -

Rashtrapati Bhawan:

The official residence of the Indian President.

India Gate:

Situated at the eastern end of Rajpath is the 42 m high stone arch of victory, renowned as the India Gate. This magnificent edifice was constructed in 1931 in memory of the Indian soldiers who lost their lives in the battlefield.

Jantar Mantar:

Located about 250 meters south of Connaught Place, Jantar Mantar is one of the world's oldest astronomical observatories.

Gurudwara Bangla Sahib:

One of the most important and sacred pilgrimage destinations of the Sikh community, Gurdwara Bangla Sahib is the Haveli (palace) where Guru Hari Krishan, the eighth Sikh Guru, stayed during his tour to Delhi in 1664.

Hanuman Mandir:

Situated on the Bada Kharak Singh Road, about 250m southwest of Connaught Circus, this temple appears to have been constructed by Maharaja Jai Singh.

Metro Walk Rohini

Metro Walk, Rohini is one of the important tourist attractions of Delhi. Located in the west of Delhi, Rohini is a residential area which comprises of flats, landscaped parks and a shopping mall called Metro Walk. The Metro Walk is a plush shopping mall in Rohini in Delhi which has a number of shops selling various items.

A storehouse of all the leading national and international brands, Metro Walk, Rohini is the hang out of brand conscious youngsters as well as the corporate professionals. Metro Walk, Rohini boasts of an excellent architecture as well. Most of the people in Delhi visit the Metro Walk, Rohini during the weekends and visit its tasty eating joints.

One of the best sections of this shopping mall in Delhi is the E zone where one can find the electronic gadgets of the leading brands. Pantaloons Delhi has even opened its retail store in Metro Walk, Rohini.

For all you shopaholics out there, who are planning to shop in Delhi, must visit the Metro Walk, Rohini for a wholesome shopping experience. The Shopping mall even has an amusement park, an adventure island and a water body where kids as well as parents can take break from their hectic tour and indulge in some fun.

Fast - Facts:

Metro Walk, Rohini is a plush shopping mall in Delhi. Located in Delhi, the Metro Walk is every shopaholic's paradise. From international brands to the electronic gadgets, the Metro Walk Rohini in Delhi offers a host of items for the buyers. Recently Pantaloons in Delhi has opened its retail store in Metro Walk Rohini in Delhi. Situated at the western side of Delhi, Rohini is a residential area and Metro Walk is a stunning shopping mall located in this area. This shopping mall in Delhi also has an amusement park which allures the kids and adults. Indian Holiday offers information on Fast Facts on Metro Walk in Rohini in Delhi.

Fast Facts about Metro Walk, Rohini:

Location :- It is located in Western Delhi in Rohini.
How to Reach :- Tourists can take auto rickshaws, taxis, buses or the Metro Rail.
Preferred Timings :- It remains open on all days.

Nearest Shopping Venues: There are a number of shopping malls in the area apart from Metro Walk, Rohini.

- ➢ Gold Souk
- ➢ CTC Plaza
- ➢ Ansal Plaza

Nearest Metro Station -: Rohini Metro Station

Nearest Airport :- Indira Gandhi International Airport

Nearest Railway Station :- Old Delhi Railway Station

Nearby Attraction:

Located in Delhi, the Metro Walk is every shopaholic's paradise. The Metro Walk Rohini in Delhi has a number of shops that sell branded goods. From international brands to electronic gadgets, Metro Walk allures shoppers from all over. Pantaloons in Delhi have also opened its retail store in Metro Walk Rohini in Delhi. This shopping mall in Delhi also has an amusement park. Indian Holiday offers information on Nearby Attractions on Metro Walk in Rohini in Delhi.

Birla Mandir :- Built by Raja Baldev Birla in the year 1938, the Birla Mandir is an important tourist attraction of Delhi. Also known as Lakshmi Narayan Temple, Birla Mandir was inaugurated by Mahatma Gandhi. The architectural splendor and the sacred deities make it an important temple in Delhi.

Mahatma Gandhi wanted that people from every caste and creed to be allowed to enter the Birla Mandir and the custom is followed till date. Dedicated to Lakshmi and Narayana, this temple was built over a period of six years.

<u>Mughal Garden</u> :- On your tour to Delhi do not miss one of the major tourist attractions of Delhi. Mughal Garden was designed by Edward Lutyens for Lady Hardinge. In its beauty and creativity it surely reminds us of the Mughals and so the name is justified. Sprawling acres of landscaped gardens intersected by water channel and fountains add to the beauty of the Mughal Garden.

<u>Crafts Museum</u> :- If you are interested to know more about the Art and Craft of India then explore the handicraft of artisans of different regions of India in the Crafts Museum in Delhi. Located near the Pragati Maidan with its rustic look and décor, this place is the heaven of Indian art and craft.

Meena Bazaar

Located between Jama Masjid and Dariba Kalan is the ancient market Meena Bazaar in Delhi. Just below the massive stairs of the Jama Masjid is the bieatiful market place. From Jama Masjid to Khari Baoli, from Chitli Qabar to Balli Maran, Delhi evokes a medieval charm and elegance. The Bazaar was built in the 1970's. The area comprises of a host of shops on both sides selling paans, burqas (veils worn by Muslim women), caps and pictures of famous Islamic religious places. Other exotic items like embroidered caps for Muslim men, local cosmetics, pictures and posters of sacred places are available at the Meena Bazaar. You can satiate your appetite with toothsome Indian non-vegetarians cuisines at the small food stalls and dotting the area.

A plethora of shops making and selling pillows, mattresses, and quilts around the Meena Bazaar is a paradise for shoppers. Nearby is a cycle market selling an exotic wide range of bicycles and their parts. Shoppers must visit Meena Bazaar in Delhi to enjoy a wholesome shopping experience.

Fast - Facts:

Location: Below the massive stairs on the Eastern end of the Jama Masjid facing towards the imposing Red Fort

When was it was built: 1970's

Special Feature:

Dhabas and food stalls serving yummy Indian non-vegetarian delicaies

How to Reach:

Tourists can avail of local buses, auto-rickshaws, taxis and metro rail to reach the market place.

Nearest International Airport: Indira Gandhi International Airport

Nearest Metro Station: Chawri Bazaar

Nearest Railway Station: Old Delhi Railway Station

Open: On all days, except on Sunday, between 11:30 a.m. to 6 p.m.

Shopping at Meena Bazaar:

Delhi is known for being home to a host of exotic shops. Shopping in Delhi is undoubtedly a unique experience. Most of the shops in Delhi represent magnificent handicrafts belonging to every Indian state. Goods are available at affordable rates. In the recent past the shops in Delhi have undergone a major transition catering to more cosmopolitan population. Delhi was a major centre of trade in the medieval era. Many of the localities are remains of the medieval period and have been well absorbed into the emerging metropolis. For tourists thronging the capital city, shopping ranks high on their priority list. Tourists can choose from a wide range of items like carpets, silks, jewellery, leather and silver ware, handicrafts and handprinted cotton. The items have varying range of prices. Shops galore in Delhi record an extensive footfall every year. Meena Bazaar in Delhi is a spectacular marketplace. The Bazaar was built in the 1970's. Shopping at Meena Bazaar is a delightful experience.

Meena Bazaar in Delhi is worth a visit. It comprises of a whole range of shops selling selling paans, burqas (veils worn by Muslim women), caps and pictures of famous Islamic religious places.

Lodi Gardens

Lodi Gardens in Delhi is located on the main Lodi Road, about a kilometer east of Safdarjang's tomb. The park was earlier known as Lady Willington Park. Lodi Gardens is all about fountains, ponds, flowering trees, blossoming shrubs, artificial streams and a jogging track. It is a popular spot visited by people of all ages.

Lodi Gardens was originally a village surrounding monuments surviving from the Sayyid and Lodi dynasties dating back to 15 - 16th c. The British resettled the villagers in 1936 in order to create the lush green gardens around the architectural structures. It was again re-landscaped by JA Stein and Garrett Eckbo in 1968 and it also houses the National Bonsai Park that has a fine selection of bonsais.

There are many species of trees, a Rose Garden, and a Green House, where plants are stored in the Lodi Gardens. Many species of birds can be seen in Lodi Gardens throughout the year. Some of the varieties are babblers, parakeets, mynahs, kites, owls, kingfishers near the lake and a family of Hornbills. Previously many vultures could be seen perched on the domes of the tombs, but their numbers have declined in recent years. It is a delight to watch the playful squirrels in the park which often come near the visitors looking for food. The garden is a sheer visual treat for the eyes during the months of February and March when winter flowers are in full bloom.

In the middle of the garden is Bara Gumbad (Big Dome), a mosque built in 1494. The garden has Sheesh Gumbad (Glass Dome), Mohammad Shah's Tomb and Sikander Lodi's tomb. These tombs boast of grand architecture inspiring the style of Tajmahal. These gardens are perfect for joggers and for people who seek solitude.

Lodi Gardens become the most sought-after picnic spot in winter and the park can get really crowded during winter afternoons. Yoga classes are held every morning in the park and regular walkers exercise early in the morning and late at night. Street lamps along the paths and jogging track make the route well lit. A walk around the serene paths of the Lodi Gardens will take you back to the times of history.

Fast Facts:

Here are some facts about the Lodi Gardens which would help you to have a quick glance of this famous garden in Delhi. Also, this will make it a lot more convenient for you.

Location

Lodi Gardens in Delhi is located on the main Lodi Road, about a kilometer east of Safdarjang's tomb.

Built In

The British created this beautiful garden in 1936.

Built By

The British planned to build it out of a village surrounding monuments surviving from the Sayyid and Lodi dynasties

Special Feature

Lodi Gardens was originally a village surrounding monuments surviving from the Sayyid and Lodi dynasties dating back to 15 - 16th c.

How to Reach

Lodi Gardens being located in the capital city, can be reached from any corner of the country.

Nearest International Airport: Indira Gandhi International Airport

Nearest Railway Station: New Delhi Railway Station

Nearest Metro Station: Central Secretariat

Nearest Bus Stop: Local buses from various points

Best Time to Visit

Winter is the time to visit this garden.

Nearby Attractions:

The places nearby the Lodi Gardens are some of the most popular tourist spots in Delhi. If you are planning for a visit to this famous garden, keep some time for a trip to these unique sites. Rich in historical and cultural significance, these places are a must-see.

Nearby Attractions of Lodi Gardens in Delhi are India Gate, Rashtrapati Bhawan, Ugrasen-ki-Baoli, Moth-ki-Masjid, Lotus Temple, Nizamuddin's Shrine and Chirag Dehlvi's Dargah.

India Gate

This 42 mt. high stone-arch of victory was built in 1931 and was designed by Sir Edwin Lutyens. It stands at the eastern end of Rajpath. It was previously known as the All India War Memorial.

Rashtrapati Bhawan

It is the official residence of the President of India. 600 meters long and 180 meters wide, it was the former residence of the Viceroy of India during the British rule.

Moth-ki-Masjid

It was built during the reign of Sikandar Lodi and is located 2 km. from the Hauz Khas. Standing on a raised plinth, the mosque has a triple-domed prayer hall and a decorated prayer recess.

Lotus Temple

Built in 1986, the Bahai temple or Lotus Temple as it is popularly known because of its lotus-shaped structure, is set amidst pools and gardens. People of any religion or faith are free to visit the temple and pray or meditate.

Nizam-ud-din's Shrine

It is the shrine of the famous Muslim Sufi and mystic saint, Sheikh Hazrat Nizamuddin Aulia Chishti. It is located about 2 km. from Humayun's tomb.

Also, Ugrasen-ki-Baoli and Chirag Dehli's Dargah are other nearby sites of Lodi Gardens which are worth visiting.

This is not all. The places near Lodi Gardens have some of the finest places to eat and shop. Eatopia at India Habitat Centre, India International Centre, Barista, restaurants at Khan Market, eating joints in Ansal Plaza shopping mall on Khel Gaon Marg and in South Extension Part I & II modern markets, the popular restaurants of Connaught Place will give a taste of a lip smacking variety of cuisines. Of course, the dishes typical to Delhi are not to be missed.

Ansal Plaza on Khel Gaon Marg, South Extension Part I & II modern markets, Khan Market, Janpath and Connaught Place are famous shopping spots near the Lodi Gardens.

Structures Inside Lodi Gardens:

There are some beautiful structures inside the Lodi Gardens in Delhi. These structures date back to the 15-16th c and are tombs and mosques commissioned by Sayyid or Lodi rulers. The architecture is typical of the Mughal-Islamic style and bears historic importance too. Lodi Gardens feature Muhammad Shah's Tomb, Bara Gumbad and Masjid, Sheesh Gumbad, Sikandar Lodi's Tomb and Athpula.

Muhammad Shah's Tomb

It is located in the southwestern part of the garden. There are eight graves inside the tomb of which the central one is said to be the grave of Muhammad Shah, the third ruler of the Sayyid dynasty. The beauty of this tomb lies in its symmetry, the crowning lotus and decoration on the domes. It is a distinctive octagonal tomb with the central chamber circled by a verandah which has three arched openings on each side. There are stone lintels along the arches of the verandah with the sloping buttressings at the corner and a chhatri on the roof over the center of each side.

Bara Gumbad and Masjid

This square tomb surmounted by a large dome, is located 300 meters northeast of Muhammad Shah's tomb. The tomb has facades and turrets and was supposedly built during the reign of Sultan Sikandar Lodi. According to the records, the interior of the tomb had stunning stuccowork and paintings. It is still a mystery whose tomb it is since the tomb had no graves. Bara Gumbad Masjid is situated on the western side of the tomb. It was built in 1494 AD as inscribed on its southern mihrab.

Sheesh Gumbad

It is located a few meters north of Bara Gumbad Mosque. It is also known as 'glazed dome' because of its beautiful blue tiled decoration which now remains only in traces above the main façade. The western wall of the tomb has the mihrab that served as a mosque. The interior of the tomb was also decorated with engraved plasterwork containing floral motifs and Quranic inscriptions.

Sikandar Lodi's Tomb

This octagonal tomb lies about 250 meters north of the Sheesh Gumbad and its features remind those of Mubarak Shah's tomb and Muhammad Shah's tomb. Located in the northwestern corner of Lodi Gardens, the tomb has a central octagonal chamber with each side opening in three arches with sloping buttresses at the corner. The chhatris of this tomb have been destroyed. The tomb is enclosed within a square garden with a wall-mosque on the west.

Athpula

It is further located east of Sikandar Lodi's tomb. As the name suggests (Ath-eight, Pula-piers), the stone bridge has eight piers, seven arches and crosses. There is a small waterway running through the garden. The bridge is said to have been built by Nawab Bahadur during Mughal Emperor Akbar's reign

Deer Park in New Delhi

The Deer Park in Delhi is an animal lover's heaven. The park came into being as the need for a green patch was required in this congested part of the capital city. The park has beautiful and well trimmed lawns with soft grass dotted with trees. A simmering water body makes it more beautiful and is the ideal haunt of nature lovers. The park is easy to reach from Hauz khas

Village, Safdarjang Enclave and Delhi Lawn Tennis Associations Courts.

The animal kingdom is dominated by the naïve looking Spotted Deer. Majestic Peacocks with their colorful feathers add more charm. Guinea Pigs, rabbits and a wide variety of birds also form part of the animal world.

With greenery all around the park is an appropriate place to relax in serenity and solitude. One can also plan little family picnics here in this park. Children's find it amusing and adventurous to come so close to nature and the experience of exploring the wild is unique.

Fast - Facts:

Location:

easy access to the park is available from Safdarjang Enclave, Hauz Khas Village and Delhi Lawn Tennis Associations Courts.

Time to visit: Open on all days

How to Reach:

Tourists can either avail buses from different points or can take auto rickshaws, taxis or metro to reach the park in South Delhi

Nearest Railway Station: Nizamuddin Railway Station

Nearest Metro Station: Central Secretariat

Nearest International Airport: Indira Gandhi International Airport

<u>Nearby Attractions:</u>

A prime tourist place itself in Delhi, the Deer Park is surrounded by other major tourist attractions. Hence a visit to this park will lead you to other nearby attractions easily. Places to be visited are:

Lotus Temple-

A very pious symbol of the Bahai Faith, this temple is an example of architectural excellence. Considered to be a holy flower, the lotus is a symbol of purity and is the Manifestation of God. This temple is located at Kalkaji in the South of Delhi.

Kalkaji Temple-

Built in the middle of the 18th century, with the oldest portion dating back to 1764, this temple is dedicated to goddess kali. Barely a kilometer away from Nehru Place, Okhla Industrial estate and the Kalkaji Colony this place turns into a major pilgrimage place during Navratri.

Nizamudin's Shrine-

The shrine of the famous Muslim Sufi saint, Sheikh Hazrat Nizamuddin Aulia Chishti, located in Nizamuddin village deserves

a must visit. It is situated close to the Humayun's tomb, not far away from the Eastern end of the Lodi Road.

Chirag-i-Dihli's Dargah-

It is the tomb of Sufi saint Nasir-ud-Din Mahmud who died in the year 1356. Located in the Chirag Delhi Village, the place can be reached by taking the Lal Bahadur Shastri Marg through the Chirag main road or one can also take the Outer Ring Road through the Soami Nagar south colony.

Hauz Khas Enclave-

Hauz Khas or the royal tank was built by Ala-ud-din-Khilji to provide steady supply of water to Siri. A lot of monuments had been erected on the Eastern and southern banks of the tank. In recent times, the area has undergone development and has emerged as one of the prestigious localities in the capital city with residential areas and shopping areas. Among the eateries the well known are those in Hauz khas village and Park Baluchi restaurant.

For shopping you can visit Panchsheel market and Ansal Plaza to name a few.

Gurdwara Bangla Sahib in Delhi

Dedicated to Guru Hari Krishan Sahib, Gurdwara Bangla Sahib in Delhi is famous as Sikh pilgrimage center. It is one of the most important historical and sacred pilgrimage destinations of the Sikh community.

Gurdwara Bangla Sahib in Delhi is the 'Haveli' or palace, where Guru Hari Krishan, the eighth Sikh Guru stayed during his tour to Delhi in 1664. Gurdwara Bangla Sahib in Delhi was built on the model of the existing palace of Raja Jai Singh in Jaipur. Later the architectural splendor was dedicated to the memory of the Guru and has been a place of worship since then and is frequented by numerous devotees.

History of Gurdwara Bangla Sahib in Delhi

Gurdwara Bangla Sahib in Delhi is supported by a legend that says - Raja Jai Singh's chief queen was greatly impressed by the spiritual powers of the child prophet, Guru Hari Krishan. During his stay in Delhi, diseases like small pox and cholera had broken out in the city. The Guru served the poor and the needy, irrespective of caste, creed and religion. With his spiritual powers he distributed sanctified water to the ailing people, which had a miraculous healing affect on their bodies. The Guru died at a young age as he took all the diseases in the city upon himself to stop the endemic.

Features of Gurdwara Bangla Sahib in Delhi

Gurdwara Bangla Sahib in Delhi opens to a large main hall which has an open central shrine. A sculpted bronze cupola hangs over it. Guru Granth Sahib, the holy book of the Sikhs, is placed at a smaller golden dome under which silk sheets are spread out and covered with flowers. The Gurdwara complex includes:

- A secondary school
- A museum
- A bookstall
- A library
- A hospital
- A holy pond

The two important features of this temple are Sangat congregations and Pangat or community kitchen also known as Guru-ka-langar.

Fast - Facts:

Dedicated to Guru Hari Krishan Sahib, Gurdwara Bangla Sahib in Delhi is famous as Sikh pilgrimage center. It is one of the most important historical and sacred pilgrimage destinations of the Sikh community.

The fast facts about Gurdwara Bangla Sahib in Delhi include:

Location of Gurdwara Bangla Sahib:

½ Kilometer from Connaught Place or Circus, near Gol Dak Khana, New Delhi, south of Baba Kharak Singh Marg.

Special Feature of Gurdwara Bangla Sahib:

The two important features of this temple are Sangat congregations and Pangat or community kitchen also known as Guru-ka-langar.

How to reach Gurdwara Bangla Sahib:

either take local buses to reach this sacred monument or hire auto-rickshaws and taxis or metro rail.

Nearest International Airport from Gurdwara Bangla Sahib: Indira Gandhi International Airport

Nearest Metro Station of Gurdwara Bangla Sahib: Central Secretariat

Nearest Railway Station of Gurdwara Bangla Sahib: New Delhi Railway Station

Gurdwara Bangla Sahib Open on: Open on all days

Best time to visit Gurdwara Bangla Sahib:

visit this place during the birthdays of all the 10 gurus (religious teachers), especially that of Guru Nanak and Guru Gobind Singh, and be a part of the festivity. Other peak festive occasions are Baisakhi and Bandi Chhor Divas (Diwali). A visit to Gurdwara Bangla Sahib in Delhi will commemorate faith, belief and hospitality of the Sikh community. Receive the blessings of the priests when you visit the Gurdwara Bangla Sahib in Delhi.

Nearby Attractions:

Dedicated to Guru Hari Krishan Sahib, Gurdwara Bangla Sahib in Delhi is famous as Sikh pilgrimage center. It is one of the most important historical and sacred pilgrimage destinations of the Sikh community. While at a visit to the famous Gurdwara Bangla Sahib in Delhi, don't miss the places nearby.

Tourist Attractions near Gurdwara Bangla Sahib in Delhi
The important tourist attractions near Gurdwara Bangla Sahib in Delhi include:

Rashtrapati Bhawan: it was the former residence of the Viceroy of India during the British regime.
India Gate: built in 1931 and designed by Sir Edwin Lutyens, it stands at the eastern end of Rajpath.

Jantar Mantar: built by Maharaja Jai Singh II of Jaipur (1699-1743), it is one of the world's oldest astronomical observatories.

Lakshmi Narayan temple: built in 1938 by the industrialist BD Birla is popularly known as Birla Mandir

Hanuman Mandir: Situated on the Bada Kharak Singh Road (old Irwin Road), this temple is of little architectural importance

Shopping Venues near Gurdwara Bangla Sahib in Delhi

Delhi is a shopper's paradise. You can visit the shopping areas near Gurdwara Bangla Sahib in Delhi and make some good purchase. Connaught Place offers jewelry, books, art, leather goods and a wide choice of Indian and international clothes stores. The important places for shopping near Gurdwara Bangla Sahib in Delhi include:

- Central Cottage Industries Emporium -Indian handicrafts and curios.

- Baba Kharak Singh Marg -the emporia of all the states of India, dedicated to each state's unique art and craft created by traditional and skilled artisans.
- Janpath -clothes, low priced gifts and souvenirs
- Palika Bazaar -electronic items.

A visit to Gurdwara Bangla Sahib in Delhi will commemorate faith, belief and hospitality of the Sikh community. Receive the blessings of the priests when you visit the Gurdwara Bangla Sahib in Delhi.

Jantar Mantar

Jantar Mantar built by Sawai Jai Singh II is an example of the scientific advancements of medieval India. Constructed in 1724, this structure lies at the heart of the city as a symbol of the technological strides of the Rajput dynasty. Jai Singh built four such observatories in Jaipur, Ujjain, Mathura and Varanasi.

During Muhammad Shah's rule, the Hindu and Muslim astrologers were involved in an unending discussion about the planetary positions. They wanted to determine an auspicious hour for the king's expedition. So Sawai Jai Singh decided to put an end to this issue by rectifying the astronomical tables.

This resulted in the construction of Jantar Mantar. So Jai Singh sent a mission to the King of Lisbon which brought back a telescope and an astronomer called Xavier De Silva. The Jantar Mantar in Delhi was set up inspired by the observatory in Samarkand.

There are different structures in different shapes in Jantar Mantar to measure the movement of the planetary bodies.

The vast red sloping structure in Jantar Mantar is the sundial or the Samrat Yantra. It is an equinoctial sun dial. The sundial cast the shadows which are used to calculate the time and the movement of planetary positions. The Misra Yantra can measure the shortest and longest day of the year. Besides this there is the Ram Yantra and the Jay Prakash Yantra meant to monitor the movement of celestial bodies.

The Jantar Mantar is therefore a reflection of the rational mind of Indians which developed years ago.

History:

The history of Jantar Mantar traces the history of astronomical interest of India. The Jantar Mantar is an astronomical observatory in Delhi constructed by King Sawai Jai Singh II. Located in the bustling Sansad Marg, the Jantar Mantar is another example of the scientific achievements of ancient India.

Constructed in the year 1724, the observatory was the result of Sawai Jai Singh's passion for astronomy related subjects. It was called the Yantra Mantra. Jai Singh built four other such observatories in Jaipur, Ujjain, Mathura and Varanasi.

Jantar Mantar was created to monitor movements of the celestial bodies. It consists of different abstract structures which were used to know the deepest secrets of the universe.

During the reign of Muhammad Shah, the Hindu and Muslim astrologers were involved in brainstorming debate about certain planetary positions. So to put an end to that and also to determine the most auspicious hour for the emperor's expedition, Sawai Jai Singh decided to rectify the astronomical tables. This resulted in the construction of Jantar Mantar

The vast red sloping structure in the Jantar Mantar is the sundial which is known as the Samrat Yantra. It is an equinoctial sun dial. The sundial casts the shadows to calculate the time and the movement of planetary positions. There is a Misra Yantra which has a number of functions and it can also measure the shortest and longest day of the year.

Besides this, the Ram Yantra and the Jay Prakash Yantra were meant to monitor the movement of celestial bodies.

Fast - Facts:

Location:

It is located in Parliament Street in Connaught Place.

History:

It was built by Sawai Jai Singh II.

Architecture:

It is an astronomical observatory which consists of different structures in sandstone to calculate the movement of celestial bodies and the planetary positions.

How to Reach:

The tourists can take auto rickshaws, taxis, buses or the Metro Rail to reach Connaught Place. Jantar Mantar is located in Connaught Place.

Attractions:

Astronomical shows are organized yearly where you can get to know about the planets and their position.

Charges for Photography: Video filming Charges are INR 25

Nearest Shopping Venues:

- Connaught Place
- Janpath
- Palika Bazaar

- ➢ Central Cottage Industries Emporium

Nearest Metro Station: Connaught Place

Nearest Airport: Indira Gandhi International Airport

Nearest Railway Station: New Delhi Railway Station

Nearby Attractions:

Jantar Mantar is an astronomical observatory, built by Sawai Jai Singh II. The tourists who visit Jantar Mantar also visit the nearby attractions of Jantar Mantar. The Jantar Mantar built in 1724 reflects the rational and curious mind of the Indians and their thirst for scientific knowledge. In the 18th century this observatory stands as a proof of the nascent scientific achievements of India. The other Jantar Mantar is located in Jaipur, Varanasi, Ujjain and Mathura.

Tourist Places near Jantar Mantar:

Rashtrapati Bhawan:

The majestic Rahtrapati Bhawan which is the residential mansion of the Indian President still reflects the glory and grandeur of British era. With its vintage charm and architectural splendor, the Rashtrapati Bhawan takes us back to the British era.

India Gate:

dedicated to the Indian soldiers who lost their lives, this 42m high arch overlooks the city of Delhi. The eternally burning flame beneath the arch keeps alive the patriotism of our countrymen.

Gurudwara Bangla Sahib:

located in New Delhi, this is the most prominent place of worship for the Sikhs in Delhi. Earlier a bungalow of Jai Singh, this is now a shrine dedicated to Guru Har Krishan.

Hanuman Mandir:

Originally it dates back to the time of Raja Jai Singh and this Hanuman Mandir is of special importance to the residents of Delhi.

Best Time to Visit New Delhi

Where to Visit in New Delhi & When
Delhi during summer: from April to June

Summers of Delhi are hot and dry. April to mid May is the best months of the season. June and July on the other hand must be avoided. The temperature during summers ranges from 25 degrees Celsius to 48 degrees Celsius. If you visit Delhi during summers, you can enjoy ice skating and shopping in the best malls of the city.

Delhi during monsoon: From July to September

During monsoon, Delhi receives moderate rainfall. Monsoons in Delhi are not usually humid and this is the best time to visit the city and explore all its spectacular spots like Akshardham, Humayun's Tomb, India Gate, Old Fort, Chandni Chowk, Lutyen's Delhi, Red Fort and many others. Delhi is at its best during this time.

Delhi during winter: From October till mid March

Winters in Delhi are usually chilly and heavy mist take over the city. However, the city remains pleasant till end of November. The temperature in Delhi, during winters stays between 12 degrees Celsius to 25 degrees Celsius. December and January must be avoided if you want to explore Delhi with ease and comfort. You can indulge in heritage walks, scrumptious food, visit holy places, malls and do many other things while you're in Delhi. Biggest highlight of Delhi during winter is Surajkund Fair, where every state of the country participates and flaunts their culture through handicrafts, handlooms, folk performances, food and other ways.

Monuments in Delhi

Delhi, the capital city of India is also its largest metropolis, which has been given several names in the due course of its history such as Indraprastha, Hastinapur, Lal Kot, Shahejahanabad and more. From the ancient times till the British rule, Delhi has been ruled by more than 88 rulers who belonged to12 different dynasties. Each one of them brought various changed in the fate and face of Delhi because of which 9 adjacent cities also came up. Most of the rulers erected one or more monuments at the time of their reign. These architectural gems are now a part of the heritage of the city as well as the country.

Memorials in Delhi
Introduction
Apart from being the capital of India, Delhi is a fascinating city with pleasant contradictions. Comprising of Old Delhi and New Delhi, the city is home to famous tourist destinations like the Laxmi Narayan Temple, India Gate, Jama Masjid, Red Fort, Rashtrapati Bhavan, Humayun's Tomb, and the vivacious shopping bazaar of Chandni Chowk. The memorials in Delhi, including Raj Ghat, Shanti Van, Shakti Sthal, Vir Bhumi, and Vijay Ghat are also very popular tourist destinations.

Raj Ghat

The most popular memorial in Delhi, Raj Ghat was set up in honor of the Father of the Nation - Mahatma Gandhi, who was assassinated on 31st January 1948. The memorial is located on the Ring Road on the way to ISBT and is about four km away from Janpath. The memorial is made in black stone and the last words of Mahatma Gandhi - 'Hey Ram' is inscribed on it. Every Friday (the day of his assassination) prayers are held. There is also a museum dedicated to Gandhiji near the memorial which houses photographs and some of his personal memorabilia.

Shanti Vana

Shanti Vana, located near Raj Ghat is the memorial of the first Prime Minister of India-Pt. Jawaharlal Nehru, after he died in the year 1964. The memorial, now a beautiful park adorned with many trees, is visited by all foreign dignitaries.

Shakti Sthal

The memorial of the first woman Prime Minister of India, Mrs. Indira Gandhi, is at Shakti Sthal. Considered a renowned statesman all over the world, Indira Gandhi's last rites were performed here and the memorial was built in her honor. A grey-red monolithic stone marks the site where she was cremated following her assassination. A prayer service is organized every year on her birthday (November 19) and death anniversary (October 31st).

Vir Bhumi

Vir Bhumi, located next to Rajghat is the memorial of the sixth and youngest Prime Minister of India, Rajiv Gandhi. The first son of Indira and Feroze Gandhi, Rajiv Gandhi was assassinated by an LTTE suicide bomber, at Sriperumbudur, on May 1991. His last rites were performed at Vir Bhumi and a memorial was been set up to honor this young visionary leader. A Prayer Service is organized every year on his birth (August 20) and death anniversary (May 21).

Vijay Ghat

Also known as Victory Bank, Vijay Ghat is the memorial where India's second Prime Minister Lal Bahadur Shastri was cremated in 1966. Prayer Services are organized every year on his birthday (October 2) and death anniversary (January 11).

How to reach

To visit the memorials in Delhi, the nearest airport is the Indira Gandhi International Airport located 23 km southwest of Central Delhi and the domestic terminal at Palam is 5 km away from the international terminal. Taxi and coach transfer is available from both International and Domestic Arrivals.

Where to Go

The idea of National Capital Region was to develop a metropolitan area around Delhi so as to divert increasing pressure of population from the region. The concept majorly focused on protecting Delhi's infrastructure from the disproportionate pressure and to carry a planned development of the region.

The major parts of NCR include Delhi, Gurgaon and Noida. NCR is the India's largest and world's second largest agglomeration with a population of 22,157,000.

Delhi has been continuously colonized since the 6th century BC. Turning on the pages of history, you come to know it has served as a capital for various dynasties and kingdoms. It was captured, ransacked and rebuilt several times. Talking about modern Delhi, it is a cluster of a number of cities spread across its metropolitan region. Delhi is appropriately titled as the City of cities. It is the largest commercial center in northern India. Delhi features a rich cultural and historic heritage, further testified by the large number of monuments dotted across its length and breadth. The major tourist attractions to visit in Delhi include Qutub Minar, Humayun's tomb, Red Fort, India Gate, Lotus Temple, Akshardham Temple and many more.

Noida is a city managed by the New Okhla Industrial Development Authority, it's where it receives its name from. This part of NCR was recognized as Noida on 17 April 1976. The inception of this urbanization thrust was put forward during the Emergency period and was created under the UP Industrial Area Development Act. Located 20 Km southeast of New Delhi, it is a foremost hub for multinational firms outsourcing IT services and the major leader like Sapient, IBM, Abstract Consultancy, TSYS International and many more have their offices in this region. Noida is replete with prime tourist attractions, some of which include the ISKCON temple, the Great Indian Place, Worlds of Wonder, Okhla Bird Sanctuary and more.

Gurgaon, the second largest city in the Indian State of Haryana is also a part of NCR. The part of NCR is located 30 KMS south of New Delhi. It is well connected to Delhi via expressway and Delhi Metro. It is the only Indian city that has successfully distributed electricity connections to each of its households and undergone rapid development in the past 25 years. From a tourism perspective, Gurgaon has a lot to offer, the prime attractions to visit while being in Gurgoan include Shiv Temple, Sheesh Mahal and the Sheetala Devi Temple. Gurgaon also connects to Rajasthan and is only 180 kilometers from Jaipur

Gurgaon Gurgaon
Introduction

Gurgaon, situated in the North Indian state of Haryana, is one of the four major satellite cities of Delhi. Thus, Gurgaon is considered a part of the National Capital Region though it is not positioned in the National Capital Territory. Home to offices of numerous MNCs, the city has emerged as the hub of IT and several other modern businesses. Gurgaon should be ideally visited during the months of February to April and August to November. Come on a tour to Gurgaon, and you will have an unforgettable experience exploring this industrial city.

<u>Tourist Attractions in Gurgaon</u>: Following are some of the famous tourist attractions in Gurgaon, which you can visit while on a tour to Gurgaon -

<u>Sultanpur Bird Sanctuary</u>:- Founded by Dr. Salim Ali, this sanctuary is positioned 20 km away from Gurgaon. It is home to

hundreds of species of migratory birds like darters, egrets, shovellers, gadwell and geese and resident birds such as teals, kingfishers, lapwings, sandpipers and demoiselle cranes. The sanctuary is decked with a museum, hideouts, watchtowers, guest rooms, family cottages, restaurant and bar.

Damdama Lake:- This tranquil lake provides tourist facilities including boating, adventure activities, hovercraft, lawns, camping site, conference hall, restaurant, bar, and motel wing.

Karna Lake :- Situated on National Highway 1 near Karnal, the artificial Karna Lake is named after Karna - a protagonist of the epic Mahabharatha. Well-appointed guest rooms and a state-of-the-art conference hall add attraction to the place.

Kurukshetra :- The land where the Bhagwad Gita originated, Kurukshetra has several tourist places like Brahma Sarovar, Narkatari Temple, Banganga, Nab hi Kamal, Gurudwara Rajghat, Kurukshetra Library, and the Crocodile Sanctuary.

Witness the various events and festivals in Gurgaon including the annual Sohna Car Rally and the Suraj Kund Crafts Mela in February, and the annual Kartik Cultural Festival in November.

How to Reach Gurgaon: Come on a tour to Gurgaon in India, using the following means of transport -

By Air:- The nearest airport is the Indira Gandhi International Airport in Delhi, located 10 km away.

By Rail:- The Gurgaon Railway Station, one of the oldest railheads situated on the Delhi-Rewari-Jaipur railway line route, is situated 3 km away from the main city.

By Road:- Buses available at the General Bus Stand Gurgaon connect you to different parts of North India like Chandigarh, Shimla, Agra, etc.

If you are about to travel to Gurgaon in the near future, Indian Holiday can help you plan your trip. For a tour to Gurgaon, just get in touch with us for the tour booking, tour packages and more travel information. Moreover, we offer prices that are among the best you can come across during your travel to India.

Best Time to Visit New Delhi

From sky-kissing infrastructure to heavenly holy spots, Delhi has everything to feed what you fancy. This capital state is always charged, but the best time to visit Delhi is October to March; this is when the weather is pleasing.

Where to Visit in New Delhi & When

Delhi during summer: from April to June

Summers of Delhi are hot and dry. April to mid May is the best months of the season. June and July on the other hand must be avoided. The temperature during summers ranges from 25 degrees Celsius to 48 degrees Celsius. If you visit Delhi during summers, you can enjoy ice skating and shopping in the best malls of the city.

Delhi during monsoon: From July to September

During monsoon, Delhi receives moderate rainfall. Monsoons in Delhi are not usually humid and this is the best time to visit the city and explore all its spectacular spots like Akshardham, Humayun's Tomb, India Gate, Old Fort, Chandni Chowk, Lutyen's Delhi, Red Fort and many others. Delhi is at its best during this time.

Delhi during winter: From October till mid March

Winters in Delhi are usually chilly and heavy mist take over the city. However, the city remains pleasant till end of November. The temperature in Delhi, during winters stays between 12 degrees Celsius to 25 degrees Celsius. December and January must be avoided if you want to explore Delhi with ease and comfort. You can indulge in heritage walks, scrumptious food, visit holy places, malls and do many other things while you're in Delhi. Biggest highlight of Delhi during winter is Surajkund Fair, where every state of the country participates and flaunts their culture through handicrafts, handlooms, folk performances, food and other ways.

Museums in Delhi

Introduction

Apart from being the capital of India, Delhi is a fascinating city with pleasant contradictions. Comprising of Old Delhi and New Delhi, the city is home to famous tourist destinations like the Laxmi Narayan Temple, India Gate, Jama Masjid, Red Fort, Rashtrapati Bhavan, Humayun's Tomb, and the vivacious shopping bazaar of Chandni Chowk. The museums in Delhi, including National Science Centre, National Museum of Natural History, Nehru Memorial Museum, Nehru Planetarium, National Museum, and National Gallery of Modern Art are also very popular tourist destinations.

National Science Centre

Located at Pragati Maidan, New Delhi, this museum is one of the largest and best science centers of National Council of Science

Museum (NCSM) with good scientific models, participatory exhibits, and interesting artifacts on display, with the aim to rouse children's interest in Science.

National Museum of Natural History

The focus of this museum is ecology. The main attractions are the various galleries visitors through the extent of the earth's natural resource, activity rooms for children and film shows.

Nehru Memorial Museum

After the death of Late Jawaharlal Nehru, the first Prime Minister of India, his residence was transformed into a museum. The museum is an enthralling place to learn about the history of the Independence Movement from the archive of Newspaper Clippings and Photographs.

There are several photographs of Pt. Nehru, giving an account of his life. Moreover, the colonial building, with its teak paneled rooms with high ceilings, spacious verandas and well-maintained gardens also draws interest.

Nehru Planetarium

Established on 6th February 1984 to promote space education and astronomy among the common people, especially the youth, the planetarium has a good sky theatre accommodating 270 viewers. It screens taped and live public shows on various cosmic topics like cosmic heritage, the solar system or history of a particular star.

National Museum

This museum possesses over 2,00,000 works of exquisite art, both of Indian and Foreign origin covering more than 5,000 years of our cultural heritage. Apart from the collections of Pre-historic Archaeology, Archaeology, Jewelry, Paintings, Decorative arts, Manuscripts, Central Asian Antiquities, Arms and Armor, etc, the museum has separate branches of publication, Hindi, Public Relations, Education, Library, Exhibition cell, Display, Modeling, Photography, Security and Administration.

National Gallery of Modern Art

Situated at Jaipur House, New Delhi, this museum was inaugurated on 29th March, 1954. The erstwhile residential palace of the Maharaja of Jaipur, the museum exhibits around 4,000 paintings, graphics, and sculptures of modern artists.

How to reach

To visit the museums in Delhi, the nearest airport is the Indira Gandhi International Airport located 23 km southwest of Central Delhi and the domestic terminal at Palam is 5 km away from the international terminal. Taxi and coach transfer is available from both International and Domestic Arrivals.

Parks and Gardens in Delhi

Delhi is famous for its lush green and manicured gardens all throughout the world. These gardens offer the visitors with breathtaking picturesque views and feature a splendid architecture. The gardens of Delhi are as unique as the history of this beautiful city. The erstwhile emperors used to spend their leisurely time in these manicured gardens. A visit to these majestic gardens is perfect for a quiet walk along with enjoying the nature. The lush green gardens of the metropolitan city are inevitable to ignore for its mesmerizing beauty and charm. A large number of people visit these gardens during weekends for enjoying with their families and friend and can be spotted having gala time.

Deer Park in New Delhi

The Deer Park in Delhi is an animal lover's heaven. The park came into being as the need for a green patch was required in this congested part of the capital city. The park has beautiful and well trimmed lawns with soft grass dotted with trees. A simmering water body makes it more beautiful and is the ideal haunt of nature lovers. The park is easy to reach from Hauz khas Village, Safdarjang Enclave and Delhi Lawn Tennis Associations Courts.

The animal kingdom is dominated by the naïve looking Spotted Deer. Majestic Peacocks with their colorful feathers add more charm. Guinea Pigs, rabbits and a wide variety of birds also form part of the animal world.

With greenery all around the park is an appropriate place to relax in serenity and solitude. One can also plan little family picnics here in this park. Children's find it amusing and adventurous to come so close to nature and the experience of exploring the wild is unique.

Fast - Facts:

Location:

easy access to the park is available from Safdarjang Enclave, Hauz Khas Village and Delhi Lawn Tennis Associations Courts.

Time to visit: Open on all days

How to Reach:

Tourists can either avail buses from different points or can take auto rickshaws, taxis or metro to reach the park in South Delhi

Nearest Railway Station: Nizamuddin Railway Station

Nearest Metro Station: Central Secretariat

Nearest International Airport: Indira Gandhi International Airport

Nearby Attractions:

A prime tourist place itself in Delhi, the Deer Park is surrounded by other major tourist attractions. Hence a visit to this park will lead you to other nearby attractions easily. Places to be visited are:

Lotus Temple-

A very pious symbol of the Bahai Faith, this temple is an example of architectural excellence. Considered to be a holy flower, the lotus is a symbol of purity and is the Manifestation of God. This temple is located at Kalkaji in the South of Delhi.

Kalkaji Temple-

Built in the middle of the 18th century, with the oldest portion dating back to 1764, this temple is dedicated to goddess kali. Barely a kilometer away from Nehru Place, Okhla Industrial estate and the Kalkaji Colony this place turns into a major pilgrimage place during Navratri.

Nizamudin's Shrine-

The shrine of the famous Muslim Sufi saint, Sheikh Hazrat Nizamuddin Aulia Chishti, located in Nizamuddin village deserves a must visit. It is situated close to the Humayun's tomb, not far away from the Eastern end of the Lodi Road.

Chirag-i-Dihli's Dargah-

It is the tomb of Sufi saint Nasir-ud-Din Mahmud who died in the year 1356. Located in the Chirag Delhi Village, the place can be reached by taking the Lal Bahadur Shastri Marg through the Chirag main road or one can also take the Outer Ring Road through the Soami Nagar south colony.

Hauz Khas Enclave-

Hauz Khas or the royal tank was built by Ala-ud-din-Khilji to provide steady supply of water to Siri. A lot of monuments had been erected on the Eastern and southern banks of the tank. In recent times, the area has undergone development and has emerged as one of the prestigious localities in the capital city with residential areas and shopping areas. Among the eateries the well known are those in Hauz khas village and Park Baluchi restaurant.

For shopping you can visit Panchsheel market and Ansal Plaza to name a few.

Garden of Five Senses

The Garden of Five Senses is much more than a mere park. This space is a perfect one to host an array of activities, inviting communal interaction and exploration as well. This project, implemented by Delhi Tourism Transportation Development Corporation, was developed to provide a leisure space to the people of the city. Also, there was a craving for a place where people could socialize and unwind. Thus, the Garden of Five Senses came into existence. It truly enhances the ambience and life of the city as well as its people. This place features prominently on the list of tourists coming on a tour of Delhi. Besides, Garden of Five Senses is also a favorite place for the locals.

On your tour of Delhi you could visit the Garden of Five Senses, one of the leading New Delhi Tourist Attractions, which is located on a sprawling land of twenty acres at the village namely Said-Ul-Azaib. This spectacular region in New Delhi is near the Mehrauli heritage area of New Delhi. Soaring birds made of stainless-steel perched on slate-clad pillars greet you inside the park. Situated on natural slope of the place, an expansive plaza attracts you up the spiral path. Across, a herd of elephants, carved in stone, enjoying a water bath, persuades exploration.

This garden is divided into separate regions. On one side of the spiral path lies the Khas Bagh. This garden was built to resemble the Mughal Garden. Slowly-rippling water flows in canals along its length. You will also find fragrant, flowering bushes and trees lined across its paths. The Central axis would lead you to a string of fountains. Quite a few of these fountains are lit up by means of fibreoptic lighting arrangements. At this place, you should ensure to visit the sculpture famous as 'A Fountain Tree".

On the other side of the garden, away from its central part, you would find the shopping and food court. At the Neel Bagh, you can enjoy water-lilies in a pool surrounded by pergols and climbing plants of diverse textures and colors. The Courts of Specimen Plants, Color Gardens and amphitheatre are some other attractions of this park.

Fast - Facts:

The Garden of Five Senses is much more than a park. It is a place abuzz with a range of activities. This is also an ideal place for public interaction as well as exploration. This project was implemented by Delhi Tourism Transportation Development Corporation. The basic concept was to create a leisure-space for people, where they can socialize and unwind.

Certain Fast Facts about the Garden of Five Senses is given below:

Admission fee: There is no entrance fee for the Garden of Five Senses. Entry is free and unrestricted.

Admission Timings: It remains open on all days from sunrise to sunset.

Preferred Timings for visit: 6.00 a.m. to 9.00 p.m

How to reach: Delhi is well linked by road, rail and air to all parts of the country. After reaching Delhi, tourists can board buses, rickshaws, autos or even hire a cab to reach Garden of Five Senses. Metro rail may also be availed of for reaching here.

Nearest Railway Station :- Nizamuddin Railway station

Nearest Metro Station :- Central Secretariat

Nearest Airport :- Indira Gandhi International Airport

What to see: The Khas Bagh, Neel Bagh, Food as well as shopping court, Color Gardens, some amazing sculptures, the Specimen Plants' Courts and the attractive Solar Energy Park.

Time needed for sightseeing: Nearly 1 hour

Photography charges: Nil

Nearby Attractions:

The Garden of Five Senses is one of the famous attractions of Delhi. However, there are quite a few places in its vicinity which are equally worthy of a visit. So, once you have visited the Garden of Five Senses, make sure to drop at these tourist attractions near this place. Some of the destinations that you may include in your itinerary are Khirki Masjid, Lotus Temple, Kalkaji Temple, Chirag Dehlvi's Dargah and Nizamuddin's Shrine.

Khirki Masjid is positioned in the heart of Khirki Village about 2 kms northeast of Qutab Minar. The main characteristic of this mosque is its unique window slits with jalis called khirki. Located on the upper point of the mosque's outer wall, these window openings were preponderantly shaped stone shields. This mosque was built in the late 14th century by Khan-I-Jahan who was Feroz Shah Tughlaq's prime minister.

In the south of Delhi, the Lotus Temple located at Kalkaji is another place which draws a lot of visitors. Resembling the shape of a half opened Lotus, this temple is built of cement, marble, sand and dolomite. Lotus Temple is open to people of all faiths. This is a perfect place for meditation and finding serenity and tranquility.

Kalkaji Temple, also called by the name of Kalkaji Mandir is a famous temple devoted to Goddess Kalka or Kali. Kali is considered to be one of the incarnations of Devi Durga. This temple draws thousands of devotees every year, especially on the occasion of Navratri. During this nine-day festival, a big fair is arranged here. The place becomes abuzz with the lively commotion of hawkers and boasts of a real carnival like atmosphere. At this temple, giving Goddess Kali a bath with pure milk forms a major part of the rituals.

Some other popular places near the Garden of Five Senses are Chirag Dehlvi's Dargah and Nizamuddin's Shrine. Hence, in addition to the aforesaid places, ensure to pay a visit to these two as well.

So, rush to book yourself for a tour to Delhi and enjoy visiting the nearby attractions to the Garden of Five Senses.

Talkatora Garden

In the Color of Grace, Tonia Triebwasser wrote, "Just as a prism of glass miters light and casts a colored braid; a garden sings sweet incantations the human heart strains to hear. Hiding in every flower, in every leaf, in every twig and bough, are reflections of the God who once walked with us in Eden." This is true enough; if one comes across the splendid Talkatora Garden he is sure to feel amazed by the overwhelming beauty of the place. Located in the hub of Delhi city, Talkatora Gardens is a popular destination for the tourists.Mainly reputed for the centrally placed Indoor Stadium, this place is a historical spot where Mughals defeated the Marathas in the year 1738. The unparallel romantic charm of this garden continues to allure men.

Three big gateways hoard the Talkatora Garden, a cosmic delight of meandering waterways, verdant stretches and vibrant flowers. The magical charm of the Mughal Gardens, with one upper and one lower, Talkatora seems to be technically well designed.

Historical Significance of Garden Talkatora:

Previously there was a tank and a swimming pool in this region. So, the name Talkatora, Tal means tank and Katora means cup.

This garden attracts tourists in great numbers especially during spring when richly hued flowers begin to bloom. Ornamented with varied flora, this garden also boasts of its playground where games are conducted and shows held.

Description of Talkatora Garden at Delhi:

These exhibitions and competitions draw mass attention and people from across the globe flock here to witness the grand pageantry. One can see potted plants, exquisite leaves, ferns and numerous other floral varieties here.

Evidently Horticulture is practiced with much efficiency and specialization over here; shows are organized for children during specific times of the year to attract their interest in Horticulture.

Visiting Talkatora Garden at Delhi:

Come Spring and Garden Talkatora is metamorphosed into a beautiful land where different hued flowers blooms. Each cries out for attention and each with its own special significance. Come and enjoy the bounty of nature and splendor of creation at Talkatora, a reputed New Delhi Tourist Attractions.

Local buses ply constantly from major points like Connaught Place of the city to Talkatora Gardens. Auto rickshaws are also available. It is open on all days.

Fast - Facts:

Verdant stretches, intermittent water-masses, vibrant flowers epitomize Talkatora garden in Delhi. Built basically according to Mughal style, Talkatora Garden is a delight to the discerning tourists. Swimming pools, three colossal gateways, centrally placed Indoor Stadium laced with thorny bushes are some of the special features of this architectural monument. The soft breeze rejuvenates a tired soul; come to Talkatora Garden and enjoy the magical charm of Mughal designing.

Location: situated on main Willingdon Crescent Road, Talkatora Garden is famous for the centrally placed Indoor Stadium.

Time for Visit: Since Talkatora Garden is open on all days; the best time to visit is from 3.00 pm to 6.00 pm.

Admission: There is no entry fee and admission is open to all.

How to Reach Talkatora Garden: from Connaught place one can avail numerous vehicles

Functional Metro Station: Rajiv Chowk is the serviceable Metro Station.

Time required for sightseeing: Minimum 1 hour is required to reach Talkatora Garden

Nearest Railway Station: the nearest rail head is at New Delhi Railway Station

Nearest International Airport: Indira Gandhi International Airport is the nearest Airport. Nearby Places of Attraction: The nearby places of attraction like Rashtrapati Bhawan, Jantar Mantar, Gateway of India and Churches.

Nearby Attractions:

Located in Willingdon Crescent Road, Talkatora Garden is a hot tourist attraction. Previously it had been a vast tank and swimming pool, this place is now a vibrant Horticultural region where one gets to see the potted plants, numerous exquisite floral variations. Nature comes close to us at Talkatora Garden. There are also numerous places of attraction near Talkatora Garden. They are the following:

Nearby Tourist Attractions in Talkatora Garden:

- Cathedral of Sacred Heart: This is a famous church located in the hub of the city. Not only the Christians but the other people too find this church an attractive place where they pray to Almighty. It is a cosmic delight for many.
- Rastrapati Bhawan is the place where Indian President stays, an important place of tourists attraction. The colossal white building is something that you would definitely admire.
- India Gate is a grand monument that is also considered to be the Gateway of India. The majestic structure is another point of attraction near Talkatora Garden.
- Jantar Mantar, a Rajput creation, is a great astronomical observatory that enables you to witness the stars and planets in the cosmos. Take delight in speculating their minute movements and enrich your knowledge.
- Gurudwara Bangla Sahib is a famous place of Sikh worship which becomes the venue for cultural association during fairs and festivals.
- Hanuman Mandir enshrined by Hanuman, the courageous fellow who brought Sanjeevani from across the Himalayas to relieve Laxmana from the grip of death.

National Rose Garden
National Rose Garden

The National Rose Garden at Chanakya Puri in Delhi is an exclusive garden for roses. The garden is famous for the large variety of roses from all over the world. At the Delhi Rose Graden you can see some of the rarest of rare and imported varieties of roses.

Fast Facts

The universally and eternally favorite Rose has been immortalized time and again by poets, painters, architects (the Mughal and Rajput frescos and tiles) in India and all over the world. The National Rose Garden in Delhi is an exclusive garden for roses. The stunning variety of roses procured from all around the world that can be seen at this park is sure to make you feel like a royal guest to the Mughals roaming about the palace garden. The fast facts on National Rose Garden Delhi are listed below.

National Rose Garden Fast Facts

Location: the National Rose Garden is located at Chanakya Puri in Delhi close to the Jamuna River and the Vijay Ghat, the Shanti Vana and the Raj Ghat.

Fast facts- Best Time to Visit the Rose Garden

The best time to visit the Rose Garden is between December and January. This is the time when you can see the flower beds set ablaze with the shamelessly beautiful roses.

Fast facts- How to Reach the National Rose Garden

The National Rose Garden is located pretty much at the heart of Delhi and well connected. You can reach the garden by hired auto or by bus.

Nearby Attractions:

The National Rose Garden in Delhi is famous for the rare assortment of roses that grow here. At this park you can find roses from all over the world, blazing in their mind blowing beauty. The nearby tourist attractions to the National Rose Garden are various. In fact most of the parks and gardens in Delhi are nestled close to each other, the National Rose Garden one of them. The Rose Garden is strategically located in the close vicinity of few of the major New Delhi Tourist Attractions.

Nearby Tourist Attraction- National Rose Garden

- Shanti Vana- Lying close to the Raj Ghat, the Shanti Vana (literally, translated from Hindi as the forest of peace is the place where India's first Prime Minister Jawaharlal Nehru was cremated. The area is now a beautiful park adorned by trees planted by visiting dignitaries and heads of state.
- Raj Ghat- On the banks of the River Yamuna, is the Raj Ghat- the last resting place of Mahatma Gandhi, the father of the nation. It has become an essential point of call for all visiting dignitaries. Two museums dedicated to Gandhi are situated nearby
- Red Fort- One of the most spectacular pieces of Mughal Architecture is the Lal Quila or the Red Fort, built by the Mughal emperor, Shah Jahan between 1638 and 1648. The Red Fort has walls extending up to 2 km in length with the height varying from 18 metre on the river side to 33 metre on the city side. This is one of the major nearby tourist attractions to National Rose Garden in Chanakya Puri Delhi.
- Chandni Chowk- the Chandni Chowk is a fascinating market planned to shine under the light of the moon. The Mughal Emperor Shahjahan planned Chandni Chowk so that his daughter could shop here for everything that she wanted.

- Vijay Ghat- Just near the small artificial lake extreme north of landscaped gardens is Vijay Ghat, the place where India's second Prime Minister Lal Bahadur Shastri was cremated in 1966.

Other Parks and Gardens in Delhi

- Japanese Garden, Rohini
- Mughal Garden
- Buddha Jayanti Park
- Talkatora Garden
- Garden of Five Senses

Buddha Jayanti Park

Buddha Jayanti Park is a beautiful well manicured garden with sprawling lawns and blooming flowers. Though relatively new in the list of parks in Delhi, it is quite popular amongst Delhites and tourists alike. This garden was built to commemorate the 2500 year of Lord Buddha's attainment of Nirvana. The significance of the garden lies in the fact that sapling of the original Bodhi tree (under which Buddha attained Nirvana) has been brought all the way from Sri Lanka and transplanted here. Emperor Asoka's daughter Sanghamitra took a sapling from the original Bodhi tree in Bodh Gaya and went to Sri Lanka to preach Buddhism. Check out the beautiful idol of Buddha that lies at one corner of the park. Buddha Garden Delhi features as one of the most coveted Tourist attractions in New Delhi.

Buddha Jayanti Park is a hotspot for young couples too. Buddha Jayanti or Buddha Purnima is celebrated each may here with great aplomb. This park was dedicated to the 14th Dalai Lama in 1993.

Fast - Facts:

Location: Near Delhi Ridge Road

Accessibility: Near to Rajiv Chowk Metro station

Time Required: 1 hour

Open On: All days from 5 AM to 7 PM

Admission Fee: Nil

Nearby Attractions:

If you are visiting Buddha Jayanti Park, we recommend you to stop by at all the other nearby attractions around Buddha Jayanti Park. Situated at an equi distance from some other interesting places worth visiting, Buddha Jayanti Park serves as a base wherein you can start to plan your trips ahead for the day. Make an early start since the park opens at the wee hours of the morning. Some of the Nearby attractions to Buddha Jayanti Park are :

Talkatora Gardens:

This beautiful garden has a historical significance. The Marathas were defeated here by the Mughals in 1738. Significantly enough the garden derived its name from the water tank that was one of the major attraction of this place.

Shaped like a large swimming pool, the tank and garden proves to be a pleasant respite for the world weary travelers and localites alike. The well maintained gardens and blooming flowers are a balm to the sore eyes. Horticulture shows are organized here. Likewise many children shows and cultural programs are organized in the vicinity of the park.

Cathedral of the Sacred Heart.

This church stretching over 14 acres of land is another nearby attractions to Buddha Jayanti Park. Located near Gol Dak Khana, New Delhi, this is one of the main Catholic Church in New Delhi. The main moral of the church lies in the universal brotherhood of man and humanity. In 1929, the archbishop of Agra laid the foundation of the Church.

Jantar Mantar:

This geometrical structure lies at the very heart of Delhi near Connaught place. It was constructed to keep track of the different celestial bodies in the days of yore.

India Gate:

This monumental gate was constructed to commemorate the 90,000 Indian soldiers who laid their lives in First World War.

Parks and temples, monuments and museums, ruins and forts all these culminate to make Delhi what it is- a perfect blend of old and new. Tourist attractions in New Delhi are many and varied.

Lodi Gardens
Lodi Gardens in Delhi is located on the main Lodi Road, about a kilometer east of Safdarjang's tomb. The park was earlier known as Lady Willington Park. Lodi Gardens is all about fountains, ponds, flowering trees, blossoming shrubs, artificial streams and a jogging track. It is a popular spot visited by people of all ages.

Lodi Gardens was originally a village surrounding monuments surviving from the Sayyid and Lodi dynasties dating back to 15 - 16th c. The British resettled the villagers in 1936 in order to create the lush green gardens around the architectural structures. It was again re-landscaped by JA Stein and Garrett Eckbo in 1968 and it also houses the National Bonsai Park that has a fine selection of bonsais.

There are many species of trees, a Rose Garden, and a Green House, where plants are stored in the Lodi Gardens. Many species of birds can be seen in Lodi Gardens throughout the year. Some of the varieties are babblers, parakeets, mynahs, kites, owls, kingfishers near the lake and a family of Hornbills. Previously many vultures could be seen perched on the domes of the tombs, but their numbers have declined in recent years. It is a delight to watch the playful squirrels in the park which often come near the visitors looking for food. The garden is a sheer visual treat for the eyes during the months of February and March when winter flowers are in full bloom.

In the middle of the garden is Bara Gumbad (Big Dome), a mosque built in 1494. The garden has Sheesh Gumbad (Glass Dome), Mohammad Shah's Tomb and Sikander Lodi's tomb. These tombs boast of grand architecture inspiring the style of Tajmahal. These gardens are perfect for joggers and for people who seek solitude.

Lodi Gardens become the most sought-after picnic spot in winter and the park can get really crowded during winter afternoons. Yoga classes are held every morning in the park and regular walkers exercise early in the morning and late at night. Street lamps along the paths and jogging track make the route well lit. A walk around the serene paths of the Lodi Gardens will take you back to the times of history.

Fast Facts:

Here are some facts about the Lodi Gardens which would help you to have a quick glance of this famous garden in Delhi. Also, this will make it a lot more convenient for you.

Location
Lodi Gardens in Delhi is located on the main Lodi Road, about a kilometer east of Safdarjang's tomb.

Built In
The British created this beautiful garden in 1936.

Built By
The British planned to build it out of a village surrounding monuments surviving from the Sayyid and Lodi dynasties

Special Feature

Lodi Gardens was originally a village surrounding monuments surviving from the Sayyid and Lodi dynasties dating back to 15 - 16th c.

How to Reach

Lodi Gardens being located in the capital city, can be reached from any corner of the country.

Nearest International Airport: Indira Gandhi International Airport

Nearest Railway Station: New Delhi Railway Station

Nearest Metro Station: Central Secretariat

Nearest Bus Stop: Local buses from various points

Best Time To Visit

Winter is the time to visit this garden.

Nearby Attractions:

The places nearby the Lodi Gardens are some of the most popular tourist spots in Delhi. If you are planning for a visit to this famous garden, keep some time for a trip to these unique sites. Rich in historical and cultural significance, these places are a must-see.

Nearby Attractions of Lodi Gardens in Delhi are India Gate, Rashtrapati Bhawan, Ugrasen-ki-Baoli, Moth-ki-Masjid, Lotus Temple, Nizamuddin's Shrine and Chirag Dehlvi's Dargah.

India Gate

This 42 mt. high stone-arch of victory was built in 1931 and was designed by Sir Edwin Lutyens. It stands at the eastern end of Rajpath. It was previously known as the All India War Memorial.

Rashtrapati Bhawan

It is the official residence of the President of India. 600 meters long and 180 meters wide, it was the former residence of the Viceroy of India during the British rule.

Moth-ki-Masjid

It was built during the reign of Sikandar Lodi and is located 2 km. from the Hauz Khas. Standing on a raised plinth, the mosque has a triple-domed prayer hall and a decorated prayer recess.

Lotus Temple

Built in 1986, the Bahai temple or Lotus Temple as it is popularly known because of its lotus-shaped structure, is set amidst pools and gardens. People of any religion or faith are free to visit the temple and pray or meditate.

Nizam-ud-din's Shrine

It is the shrine of the famous Muslim Sufi and mystic saint, Sheikh Hazrat Nizamuddin Aulia Chishti. It is located about 2 km. from Humayun's tomb.

Also, Ugrasen-ki-Baoli and Chirag Dehli's Dargah are other nearby sites of Lodi Gardens which are worth visiting.

This is not all. The places near Lodi Gardens have some of the finest places to eat and shop. Eatopia at India Habitat Centre, India International Centre, Barista, restaurants at Khan Market, eating joints in Ansal Plaza shopping mall on Khel Gaon Marg and in South Extension Part I & II modern markets, the popular restaurants of Connaught Place will give a taste of a lip smacking variety of cuisines. Of course, the dishes typical to Delhi are not to be missed.

Ansal Plaza on Khel Gaon Marg, South Extension Part I & II modern markets, Khan Market, Janpath and Connaught Place are famous shopping spots near the Lodi Gardens.

Structures Inside Lodi Gardens:

There are some beautiful structures inside the Lodi Gardens in Delhi. These structures date back to the 15-16th c and are tombs and mosques commissioned by Sayyid or Lodi rulers. The architecture is typical of the Mughal-Islamic style and bears historic importance too. Lodi Gardens feature Muhammad Shah's Tomb, Bara Gumbad and Masjid, Sheesh Gumbad, Sikandar Lodi's Tomb and Athpula.

Muhammad Shah's Tomb

It is located in the southwestern part of the garden. There are eight graves inside the tomb of which the central one is said to be the grave of Muhammad Shah, the third ruler of the Sayyid dynasty. The beauty of this tomb lies in its symmetry, the crowning lotus and decoration on the domes. It is a distinctive octangular tomb with the central chamber circled by a verandah which has three arched openings on each side. There are stone lintels along the arches of the verandah with the sloping buttressings at the corner and a chhatri on the roof over the center of each side.

Bara Gumbad and Masjid

This square tomb surmounted by a large dome, is located 300 meters northeast of Muhammad Shah's tomb. The tomb has facades and turrets and was supposedly built during the reign of Sultan Sikandar Lodi. According to the records, the interior of the tomb had stunning stuccowork and paintings. It is still a mystery whose tomb it is since the tomb had no graves. Bara Gumbad Masjid is situated on the western side of the tomb. It was built in 1494 AD as inscribed on its southern mihrab.

Sheesh Gumbad

It is located a few meters north of Bara Gumbad Mosque. It is also known as 'glazed dome' because of its beautiful blue tiled decoration which now remains only in traces above the main façade. The western wall of the tomb has the mihrab that served as a mosque. The interior of the tomb was also decorated with engraved plasterwork containing floral motifs and Quranic inscriptions.

Sikandar Lodi's Tomb

This octagonal tomb lies about 250 meters north of the Sheesh Gumbad and its features remind those of Mubarak Shah's tomb and Muhammad Shah's tomb. Located in the northwestern corner of Lodi Gardens, the tomb has a central octagonal chamber with each side opening in three arches with sloping buttresses at the corner. The chhatris of this tomb have been destroyed. The tomb is enclosed within a square garden with a wall-mosque on the west.

Athpula

It is further located east of Sikandar Lodi's tomb. As the name suggests (Ath-eight, Pula-piers), the stone bridge has eight piers, seven arches and crosses. There is a small waterway running through the garden. The bridge is said to have been built by Nawab Bahadur during Mughal Emperor Akbar's reign.

Mughal Garden

The numerous parks and garden in Delhi traces back to primarily, the Mughal legacy- the Mughals, famous for a discerning aesthetic sense and fad for magnificent architecture, were also very fond of landscaped garden. After the British established their empire in India and made Delhi their capital, they set about designing and decorating the city after their heart. Meaning, they set about designing parks and garden all over the city, perhaps to make it look more like their own capital back home (the parks and garden in England need no new applaud). The Mughal garden in Delhi are located within the premises of the Rashtrapati Bhavan, the residence of the first citizen of the India- the President.

The Mughal garden- History

The Mughal garden was designed by Sir Edwin Lutynes for Lady Harding. It occupies an area of 13 acres and is divided into three sections (rectangular, long and circular garden) and sports a blend of the formal Mughal style with the design of a British Garden.

Mughal style canals, fountains and terraces and chatris adorn the landscape of the garden, along with flower beds, hedges and a large variety of trees and flowers like roses, marigold, bougainvillea, sweet william, viscaria etc among many others.

The garden has four waterways with uniquely crafted fountains at their intersections that consist of 3 tiered huge red sandstone discs that resemble lotus leaves. The chequered flowerbeds lend an enchanting look to this wonderfully landscaped garden. With in the campus, there are many small and big lawns, like Pearl garden, butterfly garden and circular garden. The circular garden is the place which is beautified with massed segmental and tiered flower beds and is considered the best place to see butterflies.

Fast - Facts:

The Mughal Gardens located within the Rashtrapati Bhavan, is one of the most famous parks and gardens in Delhi. Designed by

Sir Edwin Lutynes, the Mughal Gardens is designed in a blend of Mughal style and the design of a British Garden. The garden is adorned with Mughal style canals, fountains and terraces. Four waterways with uniquely crafted fountains at their intersections flow through the garden. The intersection of the waterways, consist of 3 tiered huge red sandstone discs that resemble lotus leaves and the chequered flowerbeds give an enchanting look to this wonderfully landscaped garden. With in the campus, there are many small and big lawns, like Pearl garden, butterfly garden and circular garden.

The circular garden is beautified with massed segmental and tiered flower beds and is considered the best place to see butterflies. The fast facts on the Mughal Gardens in Delhi India are listed below.

Mughal Gardens- Fast Facts
Location: Rastrapati Bhavan
Designed by: Sir Edwin Lutynes

Visiting Time: 10 am to 5.00 pm everyday except on Mondays.
Horticulturist: W. R. Mustoe
Area: 6 hectares

Access: any auto rickshaw will take you to the Mughal Gardens. You can also take a bus.

With the fast facts on the Mughal Gardens in Delhi India at your fingertips, you can be content that you will be able to explore it to your hearts contentment.

Restaurants in New Delhi

As you travel to Delhi, the fascinating capital of India, don't forget to indulge in the delectable fare it has to offer. A city that loves to eat and feed its guests, Delhi is simply a food lover's paradise. No wonder, visitors are often seen tucking in the mouth-watering delicacies served with great pride in Delhi. Needless to say, Delhi is also home to many wonderful restaurants and eating joints that serve the best of Indian and international fare.

With food to suit every palate, Delhi can also be termed the food capital of India. In fact, many visit Delhi just for the amazing food it has to offer. As a result, good Delhi restaurants are always in demand. As you sit down for a fine dining experience, you can indeed rest assured of a time to remember with great delight.

The Delhi restaurants can be classified into a broad number of categories. Right from small eating joints to fancy outlets, visitors are serenaded by a good number of options as soon as they decide to pamper their taste buds. Moreover, the excellent services on offer at the Delhi restaurants also add up to a great experience for every guest.

- Baan Thai, Delhi Golf Club
- The Big Chill, Greater Kailash I
- Bukhara, Chanakyapuri
- Dum Pukht, Chanakyapuri,
- Karim's, Old Delhi
- Masala Art, Chanakyapuri
- Park Balluchi, Hauz Khas Village
- Punjabi By Nature, Vasant Vihar
- Spice Route, Connaught Place
- Taipan, Delhi Golf Club

However, there is much more to Delhi as far as good restaurants are concerned. No wonder, food lovers simply love the city.

Shopping in New Delhi

If you are planning a tour to Delhi make sure that you keep at least a day reserved for Shopping in New Delhi. There are innumerable tourist attractions in New Delhi and visiting them will surely take up a lot of time. However Shopping in New Delhi is also a very lucrative proposition. Delhi is a shoppers paradise and shopping here features on the top of the tour itinerary of many people and understandably so. So do not miss out on Shopping in New Delhi.

Delhi's importance as an important trading center has been continuously on the rise ever since medieval times. The best part about Shopping in New Delhi is that there are a whole range of markets and Shops in New Delhi. From the more recently set up plush new modern Shopping Malls to the whole sale markets to the old markets which have a charm of their own; you are at liberty to opt for any shopping destination.

But wherever you choose to shop from, you are sure to come across something that suits your liking. Take back items of your choice as souvenirs, give them as gifts or simply use them for decorating your homes.

When you are out to do marketing you are sure to be confused because there is a whole range of articles on offer that include jewelry, carpets, handicrafts, precious stones, silks and silver ware- all eternal favorites with tourists.

Each Shopping hub of New Delhi has its own distinctive feature. The feel in each of them is also unique. In fact when you Shop in New Delhi it is not just about purchasing beautiful articles, it has much to do about getting an insight into the culture of the place. Each market place appears to be a show case of the tradition of the city. Connaught Place, Chandni Chowk are great places where you can truly feel the essence of the city of the old times, and it would be no exaggeration to say that a trip to Delhi is incomplete without a visit to them.

On the other side, the modern shopping complexes are reflective of the contemporary lifestyle and society. Also mention worthy is the Baba Kharak Singh Marg where there are many emporiums.

Entertainment in New Delhi

The capital city of India, Delhi is dotted with several sources of entertainment. The entertainment in New Delhi is such that would make your travel to Delhi an unforgettable one. There are a number of tourist attractions in Delhi such as the Red Fort, Jama Masjid, Chandni Chowk, Humayun's Tomb, India Gate,

Hazrat Nizamuddin's Tomb, the Parliament House, Qutab Minar, etc. Experience the various sources of entertainment in New Delhi, while you explore the various tourist attractions in the city.

There are multifarious ways by which you can be entertained in New Delhi. While looking around the city and its various tourist attractions, you can eat out in a restaurant. There are numerous exquisite restaurants in the city, catering delicacies that would certainly satiate your gastronomical desires.

If you have a penchant for outdoor games, then you may try out your golfing skills in Delhi. The several lush green golf courses in Delhi are vast, and provide ample opportunities for the golf lovers to play a big shot.

Entertainment in New Delhi also includes the various multiplexes in the city. You can watch some great movies at these luxurious multiplexes, aided with wide screens, digital sounds, comfortable seats, etc. Light snacks and beverages are also available to enjoy while you watch the movie.

To experience nightlife in Delhi, you can visit the several discotheques and pubs in Delhi. These places come to life in the night, marked by dazzling lights, exhilarating dance and music, exotic wines and liquors, etc.

Besides, while exploring the city you can visit the several Theme Parks in Delhi, as also the beautiful parks and gardens in the city. These places of interest are ideal destinations to be entertained in New Delhi.

Weather in New Delhi

New Delhi, the administrative capital of India is a much-visited destination that also falls on the famous Golden Triangle tourist circuit of India. However, like every other tourist destination in the world, it is necessary to have a proper knowledge of the weather conditions of New Delhi before visiting it.

New Delhi is always very hot and humid during the summer months. During this period, the temperature ranges from 25°C to 46°C and the heat wave experienced during the months of May and June makes matters worse. Therefore, it is advisable to take necessary precautions while traveling to New Delhi during the summer months.

During winter, the temperature mainly hovers between 2°C to 5°C, though it must be mentioned that there have been instances when the temperature has dropped even lower. At the same time, the cold wave from the Himalayan region also makes it very chilly in Delhi during the winter months.

The weather in Delhi is very pleasant during the months of September to November and February to April. Generally speaking, the best time to travel to New Delhi is between September and April. This is the time when the New Delhi weather conditions are very favorable to visitors.

Fairs and Festivals in Delhi

Delhi the capital city of India is a cultural hub and a center of active cultural activities. Various fairs and festivals are celebrated in Delhi all through the year. Delhi's festive season begins with the Lohri and Republic day celebration in the month of January. Indian Holiday offers to give you online information on fairs and festivals in Delhi, India.

Republic Day Parade of Delhi is the biggest crowd puller and a major festival of Delhi. People from all over the country come to watch this grand event whose main attraction is the grand parade besides, the cultural events and tableaus.

Makar Sankranti and Lohri are other major festivals celebrated in Delhi. Besides, flower show, Garden festival, Suraj Kund crafts mela etc.are some of the festivals celebrated in the winters of Delhi.

Holi the festival of colors is another major festival, which is celebrated at the onset of spring. People celebrate the festival with great gusto and fanfare and apply color on each other.

Janamashtami, Navratri, Durga Puja, Dussehra, Diwali etc. are some of the other important fairs and festivals in Delhi.

Besides, the Phulwalon- ki- Sair celebrated in the month of October is the festival specific to Mehrauli in Delhi and originated in the 16th century. Literally meaning the festival of flowers, phulwalon ki Sair is celebrated by both Hindus and Muslims and is symbol of communal harmony.

Jaipur

The celebrated "Pink City" and renowned capital of Rajasthan, Jaipur was founded by Maharaja Sawai Jai Singh II on 18th November 1727. This Royal place is famed for its heritage, culture and architecture. The capital turns out to be an ultimate tourist destination due to its royal palaces, peaceful temples and striking havelis. Other than royal attractions, Jaipur displays beautiful handicrafts and fabulous jewelry.

Tours to Jaipur in Rajasthan India mainly involves visit to the numerous forts, palaces, havelis and temples and various other landmarks that testifies the grandeur of past of the city. The must visit places in Jaipur are City Palace and S.M.S. II Museum, Hawa Mahal, Jal Mahal, Jaigarh Fort, Amer, Nahargarh Fort, Central Mueseum, Birla Planetarium, Laxmi Narayan Temple and Kanak Vrindavan.

The celebrated "Pink City" and renowned capital of Rajasthan, Jaipur was founded by Maharaja Sawai Jai Singh II on 18th November 1727. This Royal place is famed for its heritage, culture and architecture. The capital turns out to be an ultimate tourist destination due to its royal palaces, peaceful temples and striking havelis. Other than royal attractions, Jaipur displays beautiful handicrafts and fabulous jewelry.Tours to Jaipur in Rajasthan India mainly involves visit to the numerous forts, palaces, havelis and temples and various other landmarks that testifies the grandeur of past of the city. The must visit places in Jaipur are City Palace and S.M.S. II Museum, Hawa Mahal, Jal Mahal, Jaigarh Fort, Amer, Nahargarh Fort, Central Mueseum, Birla Planetarium, Laxmi Narayan Temple and Kanak Vrindavan.

History of Jaipur

The history of Jaipur, which is 262 kilometres from Delhi, dates back to 12th century. Jaipur, the capital of Rajasthan expanded its name from Maharaja Sawai Jai Singh, who built it AD 1727. Maharaja Jai Singh had to come into power, when he was only 11 years old after the demise of his father maharaja Bishan Singh. Jai Singh's ancestors are Kachwaha Rajputs, who came into power in 12th century. The kanchwaha belonged to the Kshathriya or the warrior caste of Hindus. However, their origin is traced back to Kusa, the twin sun of god Rama.

The special relationship between the Amber rulers and Mughal brought the Kanchwahas real power, influence and wealth. They made alliance with Mughals and got help from them due to their rivalry with Sisodia Rajputs, rulers of Mewar that resulted in attaining a reputed place in Rajasthan. Kachwahs ruled the kingdoms of Marwar (Jodhpur) and Mewar (Udaipur) from Amber Fort.

During the reign of Jai Singh, the kingdom flourished and the capital was built around Amber Fort. It was during his period, Vidhyadhar Bhattacharya, the chief architect from Bengal, developed Jaipur as India's first ever planned city by following the principles of the ancient Indian knowledge on astronomy and

Shipa Shastra (the science of Indian architecture). It is believed that Jai Singh himself laid down the foundation on 1727.

After the death of Jai Singh in 1744, the city became interrupted by neighboring states and Marathas and Rajputs conquered most of Jaipur. Later, Maharaja Ram Singh adorned Jaipur city in pink colour which is believed to welcome the Prince of Wales (later King Edward VII) to the city, as a part of hospitality. Later it acquired the name Pink City. The colour was selected after several experiments in order to cut own the intense glare from the reflection of the blazing rays of the sun. It was also Maharaja Ram Singh, who built Ramgarh Lake to provide water to the budding and prospering. The reign is changed over to Man Singh II in 1922 and he took leadership to build schools, secretariat and hospitals. In post-independence period, Jaipur merged with Jodhpur, Bikaner and Jaisalmer to form the largest state of India with Jaipur as its capital.

Arriving from Jaipur through the narrow pass in the hills, you can see the honey coloured Amber fort-palace, which conforms to every expectation of how a beautiful Rajput forts should appear. The fort rambles over a rugged hill reflecting in Maota Lake below. The power to build such a strong and beautiful fort was built up over several generations. The Jaipur city was planned in a grid system of seven building blocks that has wide straight avenues lined with trees, with the place set on the north side. It is surrounded by high walls pieced with ten gates. The shops were arranged in nine rectangular city sectors. Jaipur city was the first sizable city in India, which was built from scratch. Even 273 years after it was founded, Jaipur city has succeeded to retain its unique flavour and old world charm. Today, Jaipur is one of the major tourist attractions of the country with its ancient temples, monuments, famous festivals and many more.

Economy of Jaipur

The economy of Jaipur has seen a boom over the last few years. While the family owned small businesses had been one of the main contributors to its economy over the past several decades, various large scale industries are now being established here. At the same time, Jaipur's family owned businesses manufacturing traditional Rajasthani goods including Rajasthani clothes, foot wear, handicraft items and the likes are now expanding with most of the business owners setting up their branches in other parts of the country.

Today Jaipur has become a hub of both traditional and contemporary industries. The skilled artisans in the city have helped in the growth of the traditional industries here and the educated youth of today is contributing towards the growth of the modern industries. It has been observed that more and more industries are now setting up in the smaller towns and cities in India as the cost of living in these places is comparatively lower than the metropolitan and the quality of life is better. The infrastructure and work life offered by such cities is also better in comparison with that in the bigger cities. Jaipur is proud to be one of the cities that has attracted several businesses over the years.

Its economic growth has also been a result of the large deposits of precious gems that are found here. It is known to be one of the largest exporters of diamond, gold and stone jewelry. In the year 2012 RBI ranked the city as the ninth largest credit centre and the eleventh largest deposit centre across the country.

Besides the various industries establishing in Jaipur, it has also emerged as a global outsourcing city gradually. Jaipur bagged the 31st position among the 50 Emerging Global Outsourcing cities in the year 2008. Genpact, Infosys and various other big companies have their BPO in the city.

Tourism Industry

It goes without saying that Jaipur's tourism has also contributed a great deal towards its overall economic growth. Each year several tourists from various parts of the country as well as abroad visit the place because of which its hospitality industry has benefited to a great extent. A number of hotels, resorts, guest houses and lodges have been built in the city and have added to its economic growth and development. It has also given a rise to the food and beverage joints here. Tourists visiting the place seldom go back without shopping and have thus benefited various other industries as well.

As per survey conducted by City Mayors Foundation, London around 2 years back, Jaipur is the 24th fastest growing city across the globe and 7th fastest growing city in India. Its annual growth is 3.4%. This computation was derived after considering several pointers of growth in as many as 300 cities worldwide and emerging on the 24th position simply shows how well the city has been doing. "The assumptions are based on past growth or decline and forecasts for economic growth by international and national statistics organizations", elaborated the foundation.

Glad at the way Jaipur is progressing, the city mayor Jyoti Khandelwal expressed his joy and also mentioned that as a mayor he still requires more power to work upon improving the city's infrastructure.

Jaipur, also known as the Paris of India, has contributed a whopping GDP of $24 billion. It is growing at a good pace and is soon expected to come at par with the other major cities in India.

Culture of Jaipur

From the time of its inception, the city of Jaipur has maintained its cultural heritage. Starting from the era of founder architect Maharaja Sawai Jai Singh till date the city has maintained its own cultural flavor. The culture of this city is an excellent amalgamation of convention and cosmopolitanism. The whole city is like its famous heritage monument –"Statue Circle" where past is blended with present: while visitors can enjoy the royal statue of Maharaja Jai Singh, they can sip a good blend of cappuccino while enjoying the majestic ambiance around.

In one word, culture of Jaipur displays its association with a royal legacy; the forts, the monuments, the palatial buildings, even the royal necropolis speaks of the heritage and glorious history of the city. Before the city was converted into its metropolitan status the pink city was simply known for its colorful history and exclusive architecture, which was based on a mixture of Mughal and Rajasthani style. The monuments, palaces, shahi baghs, and forts are the display of that lifestyle and culture, which till date is the flavor of Jaipur and its tourism.

Pink City Jaipur

The pink color of the city is one of the integral characters of the city which speaks of its inherent culture. In British India, the default the color of hospitality was pink. On arrival of Prince Edward VII in Jaipur on the year 1876, in order to welcome him with royal reception, the city was colored pink; and till date the vibe of hospitality with a royal elegance is maintained as the culture of Jaipur, and that makes this capital city of Rajasthan so special in Indian tourism because it maintains the culture of "Athithi Devo Vabha".

The City Ambiance

The city of Jaipur being the capital city of Rajasthan enjoys utmost importance in state as well as in national level. It is one of the most significant commercial centers for Rajasthan. People from all around the state come to this capital city for different reasons. While city people are found wearing formal and casual western and Indo western dresses and designer attires, rural people of Jaipur still have maintained their conventional culture of wearing traditional dress. Men with turbans and women with Ghagra-Choli is the attire culture of Jaipur, which is still prevalent with the parallel stream of urbanism.

Local Fair and Festivals of Jaipur

The culture of Jaipur is also visible in celebration of local fairs and festivals. Most of the festivals are community festivals and displays the colorful spirit of the city as well as of the entire state. These festivals are known for their local colors however they are excellent display of culture and life style of Rajasthan. In Rajasthan the prime religion is Hindu and therefore Hindu rites and rituals are celebrated here with most piousness. Teej, Gangaur are the festival where married and unmarried women pray for the welfare of their family and husbands and put the decoration of mehendi on their palms.

Since it royal era Jaipur people paid their attention is keeping pets be it is a cow, or a camel, or a donkey. Kings and zamindars used to keep elephants. In order to celebrate this pet culture of Jaipur, till date different fair are arranged. Out of them elephant fair, camel fair, donkey fair deserve special mention, and these fairs display the folk culture of the pink city

Religion plays a significant role in maintaining a religious culture in Jaipur. Being a Hindu religious state plenty of Hindu festivals are celebrated here with utmost piousness and devotion. Sitala Mata Fair, Makar Sankranti Fair, Baneswar Fair, Sitala Mata Festival, Mewar Festival, Nagaur Festival, and Desert Festival are wonderful display of cultural heritage of Jaipur.

Jaipur Literature Festival

Not only about history and royal legacy, education and patronage to modern literature is one of the integral cultural characters of Jaipur. The popularity of Jaipur Literature Festival speaks of the educational and cultural sensitivity the city of Jaipur for its progeny. In 2008, 25000 people attended the festival and had famous participants on board like Ian McEwan, Manil Suri, Donna Tartt, Patrick French, Mohsin Hamid and Tarun Tejpal. In 2010, almost 30,000 people and 175 esteemed speakers attended the program and in 2011 there were participation from 226 writers and a massive band of Jaipur residents for making the event a people's event and a gala success.

Dance and music

In general people of Jaipur are fond of their folk culture comprising of dance and singing. While Rajasthani folk lore is the traditional song of Jaipur, different dances are seen like Ghumor, Chari, where the dancers show their dancing performance with a lit diya or a pot on their head. Traditional instruments of this area are Sarangi, Ektara, Jhalar and Surbahar. However in classical dance area Jaipur has a special place for developing Kathak style of dancing which is an eminent example of Jaipur's classical culture.

Art and Handicrafts

Unless we discuss about handicrafts and cottage industry besides performing art of a place, it is never complete without incorporating these areas of creativity in discussion. Carved silver jewellery, ivory engraved sculptures, kundan and meenakari jewellery, wood craft and leather goods are all handmade and are known for their exquisite beauty. Apart from these, blue pottery, silver jewelry making, traditional cloth products like zardosi, Zari, and bandhni, Bagru block print, and miniature paining are the special artistic creation of Jaipur and its immediate neighborhood that speaks of its creative culture.

Cuisine of Jaipur

The traditional cuisine of Jaipur speaks of its culinary culture. However, it is known all over the country for its spicy taste and excellent colorful look. Dishes like Missi Roti, Dal Bati Churma, and sweets like Ghevar, Gajak, Feeni, Chauguni ke laddu, Moong Thal are some of the exclusive culinary delicacies form this pink city kitchen.

Lifestyle in Jaipur

With a wonderful juxtaposition of ancient royal heritage and ultra-modern life style Jaipur displays a cool presentation of urban lifestyle. As the old forts and havelis are used as premier hotels, similarly this old royal city has wrapped itself with new attire of modernity but its roots are still maintained in its legacy and tradition. Jaipur has radically transformed from what it looked 10 years back. The development flow is still on. It is ranked as the 5th amongst major cities on India; Jaipur is emerging at fastest pace as an urbanized metro city of Modern India.

The average lifestyle in Jaipur here has improved to global standard. The employment affluence has created wonderful opportunities for talent professionals to carve out the best work niche for themselves. Other key factors supporting such a dynamic life style in Jaipur is also due to excellent progress in all other prime domains of lifestyle. Be it fashion, best lifestyle shopping malls, events, or scope of education and celebrations, the options are endless here without compromising its quality.

The pink city of India bustles with its landscape greenery, ultra wide and maintained roads, added international airport, systematic railways, excellent cultural ambiance : in one word life style of Jaipur is indeed enjoyable unlimited.

Festivals in Jaipur

Jaipur, the pink city of India is famous not only for its vibrant culture and heritage palaces and forts, but also popular for numerous fairs and festivals. People celebrate various festivals and exiting as well as alluring fairs in every year. Festivals of all religions are celebrated in Rajasthan with equal passion and beauty. Every festival whether it welcomes or gives farewell to a season, whether it is to praise the Lord, worship trees and animals or to wish long life and good health of the spouse, it has its own importance and specialties.

Teej Festival

Teej is a great festival in Jaipur, the capital city of Rajasthan that reveals the liveliness of people as well as the rich culture of Rajasthan. It falls during the monsoon months of July-August. On this festival, the married women in Rajasthan pray to Lord Shiva and Parvati to bless them with long and happy married life. The festival of swings that is celebrated in and around Rajasthan welcomes monsoon. The swings that are decked with flowers are hung from trees. Women wear green clothes, sing songs and observe fasts for long life of their husbands. The men pray for good rain and for crop.

People believe that it was the day when Parvati reunited with Lord Shiva after a long separation. So, those who worship Parvati on this day are believed to get their blessings and their desires will be fulfilled. On this day, parents of married women send a gift packet to their daughters that includes bindi, mehandi, vermillion or henna, bangles, lahariya (a multi-coloured sari) and ghevar (a Rajasthani sweet). This gift is called Sinjara. The ladies wear the jewels and lahariya and adorn themselves with henna. As a part of the festival, processions are conducted that starts from Tripolia gate of the city and ends at Chaugan Stadium after passing through various markets.

Jaipur Kite Festival

Kite festival is one of the prominent events in Jaipur and Jodhpur and it is celebrated in 14th January, makar Sankranthi day. If you like kite flying, you should try to visit Jaipur at least once in the season of Kite festival. Kite flying is celebrated on the day of uttarayan or Makar Sankranthi to mark the transition of the sun from dhanu rashi to makara rashi. It is said that the northward journey of the sun starts this day.

On this day, the people of Jaipur take a holy dip in Galtaji, which is an important pilgrimage in Jaipur. They pray to sun to bless them with good wealth, health and good crop. On this occasion, you can see the sky is colourful with plenty of beautiful kites. As Makar Sankranthi is a government holiday in Jaipur, everybody gets a chance to celebrate the festival that increases the pleasure of the festivities. All the shops are closed and the business and other firms are shut, as everybody is engaged in kite flying on this day. Jaipur also possesses number of kite clubs who conduct kite flying competitions in the month of January. Government even organizes International Kite festival that stretch up to three days as a part of tourism where kite lovers from all over the world comes to Jaipur to participate.

Jaipur Literature Festival

Jaipur literature festival has been taking place every year since 2006. This biggest literary festival of Asia is organized at Diggi Palace Hotel in Jaipur arranging the venues in the hall of audience and gardens of the Diggi Palace. Jaipur Virasat Foundation founded by Faith Singh took initiative to start Jaipur literature festival. The directors of this festival are Namita Gokhale and Sanjoy Roy of Teamwork Productions. Even though it was organized as a part of Jaipur Heritage International Festival at the first time in 2006, it becomes an independent event within a short span of time. The number of writers and participants who attend the Jaipur book festival is increasing in every year. Jaipur book festival also conducts various debates, talks, readings, interactive activities and children workshops in these days. The other benefit is that the entry to Jaipur lit festival is free and not ticketed.

Camel Festival

Camel festival, which is organized by the Department of Tourism of the Rajasthan Government, is conducted in January every year in Bikaner. The main highlight of the festival is the colourful procession of decorated camels against the red sandstone backdrop of the Junagarh Fort. Various other things such as tug-of-war contest, camel dance, best breed competition and acrobatics are also conducted as a part of the festival. The camels with bridal bridles, jeweled necks and jingling anklets dance gracefully according to the directions of their trainers by displaying amazing footwork. You can also enjoy traditional rendezvous of popular folk performers and artistes

Famous Jaipuri Print

No matter how much fashion trends change every day and a new trend is ushered every week; demand for one thing always remains in vogue. Jaipuri Prints and their worldwide appeal never fade or fail to impress its audience and thus never go out of fashion. Jaipuri Prints are famous for the vibrant colours and patterns woven into a fabric or decorative stuff which adds an elegant touch to a house or the person donning the attire. The ancient art of floral motifs and prints stitched or painted on a fabric with immaculate precision is the novel craftsmanship of the artisans who weave magic into the handloom.

The uniqueness of Jaipuri Prints are its use of printing forms and styles of Rajasthan like Bagru prints, Dabu prints, Bandhni Leheria prints, Tie and Dye prints, Napthol block prints and the common block prints thus adding a splash of colour with hand stitches or machine made loom a chic look. The print work can be created on any fabric ranging from silk, cotton, sico and a variety of yarn fabric or loom threads. The blend of traditional motifs with modern art forms on the fabric depicting floral print, distinct stitch work along with embroidered motifs makes it so palpable. Bed sheets, bed covers, pillow covers, sarees, fabric, stitched fabric, salwar suits, kurtis, kurtas, stoles, skirts, pants, table covers, lampshades, wall hangings...the list is endless.

Jaipuri Prints range from moderate and reasonable to high value depending on the material or fabric, the embroidery or artwork and the brand value along with several factors. Nevertheless it is affordable and enhances the appeal of surroundings. So much is the craze of fusion fashion that Jaipuri Prints are in high demand which can team with modern or traditional attire. Jaipuri Prints are widely available in the market, in stores, Rajasthan

Emporium, exclusive stores and the latest rage; online shopping. Unnati Silks also specializes in crafting unique Jaipuri Prints fabrics and stitched material. It is unimaginable not to have a single Jaipuri Print attire or apparel in a person's wardrobe; if not then rush to the nearest store or simply enjoys online shopping offering a range of vibrant machine made or hand stitched exclusive designer Jaipuri Kurtis.

Nightlife in Jaipur

Nightlife in Jaipur may not have the glamour quotient of big cities like Mumbai & Delhi, but nonetheless it can still make your nightlife a little younger & exciting with its fine assembly of night clubs & lounge bars. These night clubs and lounge bars lend you an experience of Jaipur's quintessential royal life, where even nightlife has a larger than life feel to it. More or less, nightlife in Jaipur won't let you don't for sure. If anything, the experience of its royal nightlife will enshrine your memories for quite some time.

So, here is a complete breakdown of all the famous nightclubs & lounge bars in Jaipur city. All the below listed night clubs and lounge bars are considered amongst the best in entire Jaipur city.

C9 Planet
Basement, Gopalpura Bypass Road
Gopalpura, Jaipur
Located In: Hotel White Plazo
Phone no: 9414395360, 8104322907, 9001616622, 3129917

Angara Night Club
F-23-D, Malviya Indl. Area, Jaipur - 17
Tel. : 91-141-2751465/ 66, 2752707
Fax : 91-141-2751422 / 67
Swati kukar - (M)9314483211
Sudhir Kukar - (M)9829055655
Email: sudhirkukar@dataone.in, swati_jp1@sancharnet.in

Amigos Bar & Discotheque
Church Road, M. I. Road, Hotel Om Tower
Jaipur
Phone no: Not available

Extreme Discotheque
Subhalakshmi Tower, Central Spine,
Vidhyadhar Nagar,
Jaipur – 302039
Phone no: (0141) 6459999

60 ML Disc and Lounge
Hotel Rockland, 263, Frontier Colony, Adarsh Nagar, Jaipur
Phone no: 0141 2611347, 0141 4026352

Orca - The Lounge
SB 52, Krishna Enclave, Tonk Road, Jaipur - 302012
Phone no: 0141 - 4004114

Lounge Mayaa
Mirza Ismail Rd, Patrakar Colony, Pink City
Jaipur, Rajasthan 302001
Phone no: 0141 3319201 ext:127

Restaurant 3D Restro Lounge
A2 Corporate Tower, Near Jawahar Circle
Malviya Nagar, Jaipur
Phone no: 9166085000, 9166043000
Email: jaipur3d@yahoo.com
Website: www.3drestrolounge.com

Aladeen's Lounge
Ground Floor, Neelkanth Tower, Next to
MGF Mall, Bais Godam, Jaipur
Phone no: (141) 2222314, 8764241555

India Tourist Cities

Varuni Bar - Badiyal Haveli Badiyal Haveli, AC4, Gayatri Marg, Sawai Jai Singh Highway Bani Park, Jaipur Phone no: not available	Varuni Bar - Badiyal Haveli Badiyal Haveli, AC4, Gayatri Marg, Sawai Jai Singh Highway Bani Park, Jaipur Phone no: not available
The Spark Opposite Corporate Park, Ajmer Road Gopalbari, Jaipur Phone no: 0141 4001347, 0141 6514777	TC Bar & Restaurant Upper Ground Floor, Hotel Shikha C - Scheme, Jaipur Landmark: Behind Secretariate, Opposite Deer Park Phone no: (141) 4031212, 9571111456, 9582221212, 9636121212
Grunge 1st Floor, The Fern, Durgapura, Jaipur Landmark: Near Durgapura Station Phone no (141) 4121212	The Liquids Mango Hotels, Raja Park, Jaipur Located In: Mango Hotels Phone no: (141) 4166550, 9828107005 Timings: 11 A.M to 11 P.M
Indus Cambay Golf Resort, Jaipur Agra Highway Agra Road, Jaipur Phone no: (141) 3072400, (141) 3072401	Area 51 11/1, Govind Marg, Raja Park, Jaipur Phone no: (141) 4045151, 7665222202
Restro Foresto Guru Nanak Street, Raja Park, Jaipur	Wavs Lobby Level, Hotel Maharani Palace, Station Road, Jaipur

Landmark: Opposite Ramada Hotel
Phone no: 0946299985, 09232232665

Located In: Hotel Maharani Palace
Phone no: (141) 2204702, (141) 4132100

Henry's
Lobby Level, Ground Floor, Park Prime Jaipur, C - Scheme, Jaipur
Located In: Park Prime Jaipur
Phone no: (141) 2360202, (141) 2360707, 9784594016

Aza
Fairmont Jaipur, Lobby Level, Kukas, Jaipur
Located In: Fairmont Jaipur
Phone no: (141) 16420000

Lifestyle in Jaipur

People have different lifestyle based upon the area where the live and the sources available for living. Jaipur, the capital city of Rajasthan also known as Pink City of India, has a long and interesting history which reflect the lifestyle and culture of Jaipur city. The city possesses numerous world famous tourist spots in terms of resorts, historical monuments, forts, etc. The city has a population of about 3.1 million.

People from rural areas come to the city for business and shopping purposes and these people can be easily distinguished from permanent habitant of city with the help of their dressing style. Turbans of men and ghagra-choli of women is the signature of the rural population in Jaipur. The inhabitants of Jaipur enjoy a healthy living with all available sources of life. To ensure a healthy life all facilities and amenities are provided in the city for the Jaipur inhabitants. Some of the major facilities present in the city to ensure a healthy life are as follows:

Gyms in Jaipur

Some of the major gyms in Jaipur

Monster Gym, one of the best gyms in the city has been established with an aim to provide the best fitness training techniques, equipment and nutritional concepts for healthy living. The Gym is equipped with advanced technology and instruments to provide the best exercises and training on how to remain fit in your busy schedule. The fitness centre provides various fitness classes which include indoor cycling, fitness yoga, cardio fitness, indoor boxing, body pump and many more. The classes have been provided under the guidance of experts and experienced fitness professionals.

Contact Details:
Address: C-341A , Malviya Nagar,
Jaipur, Rajasthan, India

Contact Number: +919667254152

Email: monstersgym@gmail.com

Fitness Centres in Jaipur

Some of the Major Fitness Centres in Jaipur

True Fitness Gym

True Fitness Gym is one the best fitness centre in Jaipur which provide all necessary information and instruction on how to keep your body fit & fine. It is built in large spacious area to accommodate more number of people. The gym is a safe for both men and women and provides with the best fitness professionals in order to achieve you goals. The fitness centre offers a 12 week fitness program for all its members to achieve the desired body structure.

Address: B-2/521 Chitrakoot Yojna,

Vaishali Nagar,

Jaipur - 302021

Rajasthan (India)

Mobile No.: +91-9351517111, +91-9875079111

Phone No.: 0141 - 6067009

Email Id- thetruefitness@gmail.com

Shopping in Jaipur

So you are planning a visit to Jaipur? I am sure your friends/ colleagues must have already handed over a long list of items they would like you to shop for them from this beautiful city. The markets in Jaipur have an exclusive collection of all sorts of things to suit the requirement of different kinds of people. However, some of the most sought after shopping items in Jaipur include the Jaipuri Fabric, Handicraft items, Camel leather bags, belts and wallets, Kundankari and Meenakari Jewelry.

Here's a look at the markets in Jaipur and the wide array of things they have to offer to all you shopaholics out there.

Johari Bazaar

Johari Bazaar, which runs from Sanganeri gate to Badi Chaupar, is one of the oldest and most famous markets in the city. Jaipur is known for its beautiful silver and Meenakari jewelry and precious gem stones and anyone who comes here must pay a visit to this market to get a glimpse of the ornamental trinkets and jewels this place has to offer. The Bazaar is full of jewelry stores that offer beautifully carved silver and gold neck pieces, ear rings, bangles, pendants, rings and anklets. The jewelry here is embedded with diamonds, rubies and pearls cut in a special manner. The Kundankari and Meenakari work done here is simply matchless

The market is ideal for wedding shopping as besides jewelry stores the market also encompasses shops that offer a wide range of lehengas, saris and designer suits. Traditional Rajasthani saris and dress material is also available here. It is suggested to park your car at a good distance from the market to avoid rush. You may also try various Rajasthani cuisines while shopping in this market. The Laxmi Mishtan Bhandar situated here is famous for its delicious desserts.

Bapu Bazaar

Bapu Bazaar, which runs from New gate to Ajmeri gate, offers a wide variety of Rajasthani kurtis, dupattas, skirts, handbags, jutis and artificial jewelry. It is especially famous for Sanganeru and Bagru print garments. The best thing about this market is that everything is reasonably priced. Even better for you, if you are good at bargaining! It also includes shops that offer a wide range of wedding lehengas and saris. A number of cosmetic shops, beauty parlors, heena shops and boutiques are also located in this market, thus making it a favorite amongst the women.

People flocking around the Pani puri, chaat and pakora stalls to enjoy these mouthwatering snacks is a common sight here. Sweet supari shops at Bapu Bazaar are also quite popular.

Tripolia Bazaar

Tripolia Bazaar begins from Badi Chaupar and ends at Chhoti Chaupar. It is known for selling beautiful pieces of copper, brass, steel and aluminum pottery. The market is ideal for festive shopping. All kinds of goods required during the festival season are available here. You will find various decorative items and also several gift options in this market – from showpieces to dry fruits they have it all and that too at reasonable rates. The market also has shops that sell plastic goods, toys, stationary, cosmetics, metal antique accessories, watches, shoes, spices, pickles, bags and various other daily needs items.

Tripolia Bazaar is illuminated with lights during Dhanteras and Diwali and is also the busiest during these days. It encompasses two old sweet shops that offer delicious delicacies; Motichoor Ke Laddoo available here are definitely worth a try.

Chaura Rasta

Located near Tripolia Bazaar, Chaura Rasta runs from Tripolia gate to New gate. This market is quite like the Nai Sarak in Old

Delhi. It has several book stores and publishing houses that sell academic books, novels and various other kinds of books. The market has a host of stationary shops as well where you may shop for note books, registers, pens, pencils, colors, rubber stamps and other similar items. Several printing presses are also located here.

Apart from this, you can also shop for branded watches and glasses at Chaura Rasta. Walking past the Chaura Rasta, you are also likely to come across shops that sell flower pots and toys made of clay.

Kishanpol Bazaar
Kishanpol Bazaar spread between Ajmeri gate and Chhoti Chaupar, is another popular market in Jaipur. You would be able to find a variety of things in this market. Whether you are looking for decorative items such as paintings, necessary grocery items or household furniture you will find everything in this stretch. Kishanpol Bazaar also has a couple of good sports shops where you can shop for various sports items including cycles for kids as well as adults. Various handicraft items are also available in the market.

Chaandpol Bazaar

Situated between Chaandpol gate and Chhoti Chaupar, Chaandpol Bazaar is famous for its scrumptious pickles, spices and ghee. The market area is filled with the aroma of various Indian spices. Several restaurants offering luscious Rajasthani cuisines are also located in this market. If you want to taste special Rajasthani food then you must visit Chaandpol Bazaar. Here, you would not only be able to taste a variety of Rajasthani cuisines but would also get the opportunity to take along some special spices to add flavor to your home cooked food.

The market also has a number of readymade garment shops, exclusive handicraft items and beautiful marble statues.

Hawamahal Bazaar

This Bazaar is spread between Badi Chaupar and Silver Mint market. It is mostly visited by tourists – both Indian as well as foreign. Tourist buses usually stop at Hawamahal Bazaar and thus the rates of this market are comparatively higher. Various antique pieces made from brass, wood and cooper are available in this market. Shopkeepers mostly keep these beautiful decorative items by the road side to attract the tourists. The market is also loaded with traditional Rajasthani dresses, bags, sandals and accessories. Handmade paintings and various handicraft items are also available in this market. Exclusive

Jaipuri items available here are sure to entice you and you are likely to buy a thing or two even if you enter the market with the sole intention of window shopping.

Mirza Ismial Road (M I Road)

M I road is one of the most famous destinations for shopping in Jaipur. Here you will find numerous shops and emporiums selling a wide variety of goods. You can shop for blue pottery, cotton rugs, textiles, brass work, Carpets, dresses and colorful cotton wraps. It would not be wrong to mention that M I road is a place where you will find all the specialties of Jaipur at one single place.

Kazane Walon Ka Raasta

It is situated on the western side of Baba Harish chandra Marg. It is famous for sculptures carved out of stone, and are available in all sizes. Some of the shops that are best for shopping in Jaipur are government approved emporiums, Rajasthali and Handloom house. Markets in Jaipur are usually closed on Sundays.

Besides these there are several other markets including the Indira Bazaar, Nehru Bazaar, Lalji Saand Ka Rasta, Ramganj Bazaar, Gangauri Market and Bhindon Ka Rasta that are frequently visited by the locals as well as the tourists.

Public Transport in Jaipur

Jaipur the Pink City is counted amongst the most liked and preferred tourist destination. People from various cities or even countries having different cultural background visit Jaipur and relish the architectural history and huge royal forts of ancient India. As the city is getting advanced, the facilities have also increased may it be in terms of stay in lavish hotels, shopping in malls, or the most important of all – transportation. With the presence of different modes of traveling, it becomes easy to explore the beautiful views of the Pink City.

Jaipur with its advancement has become easily approachable and connected to the nearby cities around it. Modes like auto rickshaw, cycle rickshaw, local buses and taxis make the life easier for commuters. Within city, people prefer to travel through auto rickshaws which are the most convenient and cheaper mode for short distances. With the code color of green and yellow, the rickshaws run on CNG for Eco-friendly purpose. The auto rickshaws run on the planned fare chart which varies from travel distance to the destination. This meter system is fair deal for the drivers as well as passengers. For minimum distance of 3 km traveled, the fare charge will be Rs.17. this is the minimum amount for minimum distance that can be traveled.

RSRTC

Rajasthan State Road Transport Corporation is the government corporation that was established in October 1964 under the Road Transport Act. With covering around thousands or more kilometers and carrying lakhs of passengers every day, their services have served people with comfort, time savior in term of commuting and facility. Their services provide best quality service and the routes that are being followed have connected various places very conveniently. The various measure that are being taken to serve people with the best are effective cost of traveling, online or on-site reservation of tickets, less commuting time from place to place, regular and well scheduled travel timings etc. Facility of online inquiry is available through their website and even the contact numbers are available for any sort of clarification that a passengers need to clear.

Contact numbers:	Contact details:
Control room, Jaipur(24hrs) – 0141- 2373044	Head office
Central bus stand, Jaipur – 0141- 2207906, 2207912, 2204445, 2207913, 2207914.	Parivahan Marg, Chaumu House Jaipur (Rajasthan), 302001
Enquiry – 0141- 2670159, 2574645, 2297574	Contact Number: 0141-2373043, 44, 51, 54, 9549456745
Accident cell – 0141- 22207908	Email: cmd.rsrtc@gmail.com
	Website: www.rsrtc.rajasthan.gov.in

Transporters in Jaipur

There are variety of transporter companies that have been serving their people since many years. They not only provide comfort to the users but in very affordable prices, the services are of excellent level and also on time. Some of the transporter service providers give 24 hours of service. So at any point of time when someone seeks for need, can contact them through online facility or even calls.

Golden Transport Corporation

B-4, behind of Punjab motors store, Transport Nagar, Jaipur – 302003

Contact: 0141- 4362307

Sejal Transport

Near Metro Hospital, Sirsi Road, Sirsi Road, Jaipur – 302021

Contact: 0141- 4652467

Wipro Packers and Movers

Shop No 8, New Chungi Naka, Ajmer Road, Jaipur – 302001

Contact: 0141- 4362839

Jaipur Roadways

A-23, Agra Rd, Transport Nagar, Jaipur – 302003

Contact: 0141- 2640975

Globe Transport Co. Pvt. Ltd.

Td-10, Transport Nagar, Jaipur – 302003

Contact: 0141-2641606

Buses from Jaipur

- Rajasthan State Road Transport Corporation, Non AC, Dep - 06:30, Arr – 12:00, Fare – Rs.244
- Rajasthan State Road Transport Corporation, Non AC, Dep - 07:40, Arr – 13:15, Fare – Rs.244
- Rajasthan State Road Transport Corporation, AC, Volvo, Dep - 08:30, Arr - 13:00, Fare – Rs.491
- Rajasthan State Road Transport Corporation, AC, Seater, Dep - 13:01, Arr -18:00, Fare – Rs.424
- Rajasthan State Road Transport Corporation, AC, Seater, Dep - 15:30, Arr - 20:30, Fare - Rs.419
- Uttar Pradesh State Road Transport Corporation, AC, Volvo, Dep - 17:00, Arr - 22:25, Fare Rs.484.

Jaipur Bus Routes

There is a well-connected network that runs through the cities that are near Jaipur city. With constructions of National Highways, the transport medium has become quite easy and convenient for regular traveling. The buses run under RSRTC over the routes of NH-8 that connects Jaipur with Delhi and then Mumbai, Jaipur is connected to Kota via NH-12 and to go to Agra and Bikaner the buses follow the route of National Highway 11. The booking for the tickets is easily available online on the website.

Jaipur Low Floor Buses

As the city develops the needs and requirements of people also increase at the same time. Like many other cities, Jaipur has become one of the fastest growing cities at present. And to fulfill the basic need of everyday commuters there were special low floor buses that were launched in this city like in Delhi, Chandigarh and many more. Under the Government rule, these low floor buses run on CNG gas which is welfare of humans and well as environment. The buses include AC as well Non-AC buses with variation in minimum fare rates depending on the service used. Known with the name of BRTS it is done under the joint venture of JNN and JDA. These buses have been specially designed by taking in care the old people, physically challenged and unhealthy passengers too. Low floor makes t easy to climb in. the engine are has been shifted to rear part so as to avoid any interference with passenger's way. Automated doors ensure complete safety of passengers and make it safe enough for every age group.

Route for Jaipur Low floor buses

Based on the different service provider of low floor buses, there are specific routes that have been set for passenger convenience. The red low floor bus (AC) and the green low floor bus (Non-AC) follow different routes.

- Route 1 - Todi to Badi Chopar
- Route 2 - Bhankrota to Chandpole
- Route 3 - Pratap Nagar to Choti Chopar
- Route 4 - Kanota to Sindhi Camp
- Route 5 - Collectorate to kunda
- Route 6 - Malviya Nagar to Govindpura
- Route 7 - Heerapura to Transport Nagar
- Route 9 - Daadi ka Fatak to Agarwal Farm

Circular routes in Jaipur

- ➤ Route 8 - Jagatpura to Jagatpura
- ➤ Route 9 - Dadi ka Phatak to Dadi Ka Phatak

Contact:

Jaipur Development Authority

Ram Kishor Vyas Bhawan, Indra Circle, Jawaharlal Nehru Marg, Jaipur- 302004

Contact number: 0141- 2569696

Toll Free Number: 1800 180 6695, 1800 180 6696

Email: public@mailjda.org

Jaipur Airport

JAI known as Jaipur Airport is the only international airport in Rajasthan. It is located in southern suburb which is approximately 13 km from Jaipur. Jaipur Airport though international, has many features of Rajasthani culture and aspects that can be seen in its structure. Jaipur Terminal 1 is reserved for domestic and International flights and is 13-14 km away from Jaipur whereas Jaipur Terminal 2 is used only for domestic purposes and is 7 km away from the city.

Airport Code (IATA)- JAI

ICAO Code- VIJP

Corporate Address- Civil Airport, Sanganer, Jaipur, Rajasthan, India,

Contact Number- 0141 2550623

Email id- apdjpr@aai.aero

Jaipur Airport is well connected with all major cities and states of India like Delhi, Mumbai, Udaipur, Bengaluru and Ahmadabad. Starting as an domestic airport only, the international certification was done on 29 December 2005.The structure welcomes the visitors with its entrance gate made of sandstone and stones from Dholpur (a place famous for its best quality stone). With fascinating interiors that showcase Rajasthani paintings in its ultra modern infrastructure of glass and iron, Jaipur Airport is a blend of vintage and modernity. The terminals are beautified further with a paved area with palm trees queued on either side. The Eco friendly factor of the temperature maintenance with the help of trees also adds an aesthetic appeal. Jaipur Airport also uses many energy saving methods and survives on natural resources.

The modernity of the building lies in the transparent glass walls with an automated shield that maintains the temperature and also the flow of light thus being energy efficient in terms of lighting. Jaipur Airport spreads over a vast area of twenty eight lakh square meters with an accommodation of 14 A320 aircraft.

The certification in International and Domestic terms are based on its tie up with many airlines listed below.

- Indian Airlines
- Air Deccan
- Jet Airways
- Air Sahara
- Go Air
- Kingfisher Airlines
- Indigo
- JetKonnect
- Oman Air
- Spice Jet
- Air India Express
- Air Costa and many more.

The main operations are done through Terminal 1 and Terminal 2 with 14 check in counters at Terminal 2. The new terminal building is designed in a manner to handle 28 flights in a day to 16 destinations. Every airline is provided with three check in counters to speed the process and value the time of passengers. Aerobridges and in-terminus buses are provided along with modern conveyor belts that facilitate the passengers to lift their baggage, an advantage for elderly and pregnant women.

Apart from its contribution to the earth being energy efficient, it also contribute to its visitors with the following facilities:-

- Wi-fi Connectivity
- 3 VIP Lounges
- Souvenir Shops
- ATM's
- Cash Machines
- Foreign Exchange
- Car Rentals
- Taxi Service
- Luggage Storage
- Lockers
- Showers
- Vending machines
- Child Care Room
- General and Premium car Parking
- Entertainment
- Lost and Found property
- Food and Dining

The cargo terminal with an area of 700 square meters facilitates the cargo terminal facility which is basically provided by Rajasthan Small Scale Industries Co. Ltd. Blue Dart Aviation is related for this facility.

Following are some **taxi services** that the Airport offers to its passengers that are available almost 24/7

Taxi Services Jaipur

Contact- 09314118804

MY Cab

Contact- 0141 5000000

Pinkcity Radio taxi Private Ltd.

Contact- 0141 5108888

Jaipur Travels

Contact- 0141 2317957

Taxi Rajasthan

Contact- 09828145651

Also near the Airport, many Hotels are lined up for the comfort of Passengers, some of which are:-

The Lalit

Address- 2b & 2c, Near Jawahar Circle, Jagatpura Road, Malviya

Nagar, Jaipur

Contact- 0141 4362849

Hotel Sidharth Place

Address- A 18, Near Gold Souk, Jawahar Circle, Saraswati Nagar, Malviya Nagar, Jaipur

Contact- 01414652133

Royal Estate Hotel

Address- 32/101, Near Ganga Jamna, Swarn Path- Shipra Path, Mansarovar, Jaipur.

Contact- 0141 4651742

Hotel Dev Villas

Address- Gujar ki Thadi, Near HPCL Petrol Pump, Main Gopalpura Bypass Road, New Aatish Market, Jaipur.

Contact- 0141 4361110

Jaipur Mariott Hotel

Address- Near Jawahar Circle, Ashram Marg, Tonk Road, Jaipur.

Contact- 0141 4567777

Despite many ultra modern facilities, many changes are still being incorporated in Terminal 2 to extend its runway which can accommodate Boeing 747 and Airbus 320 and also its collaboration with Singapore Airlines, Gulf Airlines and Biman Airlines. With these few additions, the glory of Jaipur Airport will boom thus adding more international destinations to its list of operations.

Jaipur Metro

One of the major engineering achievements of humankind is introduction of Metro Rail into existence. Not only it has influenced major parts of world by functioning in various European and Asian countries but is further motivating many other regions to bring it use. Metro service has served people with comfort in various terms. In India the metro service was first introduced in Kolkata in 1984.

Later DMRC made metro service functional in capital city of India – Delhi in year 2002 in month of December. Unprecedented growth of private vehicles day by day was a major issue for which Metro service has shown a major effect. Its been realized that metro service has promoted people to use this facility for regular travel, which not only reduces journey time but also reduces per day fuel consumption and air pollution.

Other than Kolkata, Delhi and Bangalore, many other cities have been proposed with Metro Railway. Jaipur city capital of Rajasthan is expected to become India's fourth Metro Rail system after other 3 cities. The construction part of Metro Rail had started in year 2010 with line comprising from Mansarovar upto Chandpole Bazaar. The Metro rail service in Jaipur is being executed by JMRC i.e. Jaipur Metro Rail Corporation.

Jaipur Metro Project

It is a corporation working under Government of Rajasthan. According to the JMRC authorities, the train is expected to start in early 2014 year after all the trials and safety measures being taken in 2013. The whole project is supposed to cover around 29 stations in Jaipur which will comprise of 2 lines which are Green Line (Phase – I) and Orange Line (Phase – II). At present the construction process is undertaken for Green Line Phase – I route of Jaipur Metro Rail which will be running from Mansarovar to Chandpole and Orange Line i.e. Phase – II will connect Sitapura Industrial Area to MI Road.

The road networks of Jaipur have been facing traffic congestion during peak hours. Due to growing population and development of city demands development even in terms of transportation facilities. After Delhi has experience a very positive response after introduction of Metro Rail by DMRC, Jaipur is another city which would be experience relief in terms of aggravated congestion on roads and streets due to increase in population. Addition of metro service will propose people to travel through public transport rather than private transportation methods.

This will not only make their life easier in terms of less commuting time and stress free travel but will also contribute to healthy surrounding and environment by reducing less pollution emission. It will be justified to say that Metro Rail is one of the most effective technologies that has been introduced in various cities in India which is a very major contribution to human kind in today's busy life. In every way it has proved itself worth of every effort being made for its growth in many other cities too.

Very soon Jaipur the Pink City will be blessed with the plan of Metro Rail that will be running across the city's various parts connecting them through two phase of connecting lines and millions of people will experience relief in terms of travel in the fast growing city of Rajasthan.

The Jaipur metro, considered as the 'fastest built metro', was opened to the public on 3rd June, 2015. Its maiden journey was flagged off by the CM Smt. Vasundhra Raje. The metro being a symbol of cultural and economical growth, also encouraged equality to women at work with about 30% of women workers in the staff.

Jaipur Railway Station

The Jaipur Railway Station, serves approximately 35,000 passengers per day on it's seven platforms. The connectivity to the station is through various major cities of the country like Delhi, Mumbai, Chennai, Kolkata, Chandigarh, Indore, Bhopal, Lucknow, Kanpur, Patna, Hyderabad, Kota etc. There are three major lines that pass through Jaipur which are Delhi-Ahmadabad Line, Sawai Madhopur and Jaipur–Sikar. One of India's most famous trains known as The Palace on Wheels also makes way through this station.

The station code of Jaipur Railway Station is –JP

Enquiry number is 139.

Sub-Stations Under Jaipur Railway Station

Gandhinagar Jaipur Railway Station is another railway station that is located in Jaipur City. Many of the train networks follow this route to pass by or to arrive from this railway station.

The station code for Gandhinagar Jaipur Railway Station is GADJ and the name is known as Gandhinagar Jpr.

Gator Jagatpura Railway Station located in Jaipur, Sanganer is one of the railway routes of the north western India. The nearby stations which are situated around this railways station are Durgapur station and Gandhinagar Jpr.

The station code of Gator Jagatpura Railway Station is GTJT

Durgapur Railway Station located near Gator Jagatpura station is another railway station of north western railway networks located in Jaipur. The nearby cities around this railway station are Railway colony durgapura, Barkat Nagar and Chatrsal Nagar.

The station code Durgapur Railway Station is DPA

Dahar Ka Balaji Railway Station is located in Jaipur, Rajasthan. This station is located right after Jhotwara.

The station code for Dahar Ka Balaji Railway Station is DKBJ.

Bais Godam Railway Station is located 3 kms away from Jaipur Railway Station

The station code for Bais Godam Railway Station is BSGD.

Kanakpura Railway Station is situated near Sirsi road which is around 4 Km away from Khatipura Mod.

The station code for Kanakpura Railway Station is KKU.

Jaipur Railway station is very close to City Wall of Jaipur, Vidhan Sabha and Statue circle. Jaipur Railway Station is also lined with many restaurants around its vicinity thus making travel easier for tourists and also safe getaways

Trains from Jaipur

Jaipur is a major international tourist station. People from all over the world visit this magnificent city to unravel the architectural brilliance and the grandeur of not just the city but also the traditions and customs which have been carried forward since many ages. Connectivity to any city is major issue and the better the transport, the better growth of tourism. Find out the various train routes to Jaipur from major Indian cities below;

Trains from Jaipur to Delhi

- Ajmer Shatabdi Special; Train No. 04042; Depart time 17:50; Arrival time 22:40; Wednesday
- Jaipur Delhi Settigunta Special; Train No. 09721; Depart time 06:00; Arrival time 10:30; All days

- Ajmer Shatabdi; Train No. 12016; Depart time 17:50; Arrival time 22:40; All days except wed.
- Delhi Garibrath; Train No. 12216; Depart time 06:50; Arrival time 12:10 ; Mon, Wed, Thus, Sat.
- Ajmer Jammu Express; Train No. 12413; Depart time 16:30; Arrival time 22:10; All days.
- Ala Hazrat Express; Train No. 14312; Depart time 08:00 – Arrival time 14:35 – Mon, Tue, Fri, Sun.

Trains from Jaipur to Mumbai

- Jaipur Pune Shatabdi Express– Train No. 09730 - Depart time 09:00 – Arrival time 06:30 – Saturday
- Delhi Mumbai Gondia Rath – Train No. 12215 - Depart time 14:25 – Arrival time 08:10 – Mon, Tue, Thus, Sat.
- Jaipur Pune Settigunta Express - Train No. 12940 - Depart time 09:05 –Arrival time 05:15 – Tue
- Jaipur Mumbai Superfast - Train No. 12956 - Depart time 14:10 –Arrival time 07:50 – All days
- Aravali Express - Train No. 19708 - Depart time 08:30 – Arrival time 06:45 – All days.
- Jaipur Mumbai Shrungavarpukta Express - Train No. 12980 - Depart time 20:40 – Arrival time 14:30 – Mon, Wed, Fri.

Trains from Jaipur to Agra

- Ajmer Af Intercity– Train No. 12196 - Depart time 16:55 – Arrival time 21:30 – All days
- Jodhpur Kolkata Superfast – Train No. 12308 - Depart time 02:10 – Arrival time 06:35 – All days
- Ananya Express - Train No. 12316 - Depart time 09:05 – Arrival time 15:50 – Tue
- Jaipur Mumbai Superfast - Train No. 12956 - Depart time 14:10 –Arrival time 07:50 – Mon.
- Ajmer Sealdah Express - Train No. 12988 - Depart time 14:45 – Arrival time 19:30 – All days.
- Marudhar Express - Train No. 14854 - Depart time 15:50 – Arrival time 21:00 – Mon, Thus, Sat.
- Ranchi Garib Nawaz - Train No. 18632 - Depart time 21:35 – Arrival time 03:25 – Sat.

Trains from Jaipur to Jodhpur

- Kolkata Jodhpur Express– Train No. 12307 - Depart time 01:00 – Arrival time 07:00 – All days
- Mandor Express – Train No. 12461 - Depart time 02:15 – Arrival time 08:00 – All days

- Rajasthan S Krant - Train No. 12463 - Depart time 03:25 – Arrival time 09:10 – Mon, Thus, Sat.
- Ranthambore Express - Train No. 12465 - Depart time 16:16 –Arrival time 22:30 – All days.
- Delhi Jaisalmer Express - Train No. 14059 - Depart time 23:20 – Arrival time 16:18 – All days.
- Guwahati Barmer Bikaner Express - Train No. 15632 - Depart time 23:25 – Arrival time 05:05 – Fri, Sun.
- Puri Jodhpur Express - Train No. 18473 - Depart time 06:15 – Arrival time 13:05 – Fri.

Trains from Jaipur to Kota

- Jaipur Indore Settigunta Special – Train No. 09728 - Depart time 20:40 – Arrival time 00:01 – Tue.
- Jaipur Pune Settigunta Special – Train No. 09730 - Depart time 09:00 – Arrival time 12:50 – Sat.
- Hanumangarh Kota Special - Train No. 09733 - Depart time 05:25–Arrival time 09:20 – All days.
- Dayodaya Express - Train No. 12182 - Depart time 17:25 – Arrival time 21:05 – All days.
- Intercity Express - Train No. 12466 - Depart time 10:55 – Arrival time 14:45 – All days.

- Jaipur Mumbai Superfast - Train No. 12956 - Depart time 14:10 – Arrival time 17:25 – All days.
- Jaipur Indore Express - Train No. 12974 - Depart time 21:10 – Arrival time 00:25 – Fri, Sun.

Trains from Jaipur to Ajmer

- Ajmer Shatabdi Special – Train No. 04041 - Depart time 10:40 – Arrival time 12:45 – Wed.
- Jaipur Ajmer Intercity – Train No. 09622 - Depart time 14:15 – Arrival time 16:10 – All days.
- Jaipur Ajmer Special - Train No. 09756 - Depart time 17:35 - Arrival time 20:15 – All days.
- Haridwar Ajmer Special - Train No. 09639 - Depart time 08:28 – Arrival time 11:30 – Mon, Wed, Sat.
- Ibadat Express - Train No. 12395 - Depart time 13:10 – Arrival time 15:20 – Thus.
- Jammu Ajmer Express - Train No. 12414 - Depart time 09:31 – Arrival time 12:20 – All days.
- Ashram Express - Train No. 12916 - Depart time 20:45 – Arrival time 23:00 – All days.

Trains from Jaipur to Udaipur

- Ananya Express – Train No. 12315 - Depart time 17:20 – Arrival time 03:00 – Fri.
- Gwalior Udaipur Shrungavarpukta Express – Train No. 12965 - Depart time 22:03 – Arrival time 06:10 – All days.

Trains from Jaipur to Ahmedabad

- Delhi Mumbai Gondia Rath – Train No. 12215 - Depart time 14:25 – Arrival time 01:20 – Mon, Tue, Thus, Sat.
- Ashram Express – Train No. 12916 - Depart time 20:45 – Arrival time 07:40 – All days.
- Ahmendabad Shingaji Rajdhani - Train No. 12958 - Depart time 00:35 - Arrival time 10:05 – All days.
- Haridwar Ahmedabad Mail - Train No. 19106 - Depart time 04:55 – Arrival time 18:40 – All days.
- Aravali Express - Train No. 19708 - Depart time 08:30 – Arrival time 22:10 – All days.
- Delhi Porbandr Express - Train No. 19264 - Depart time 13:50 – Arrival time 02:55 – Mon, Thus.

Trains from Jaipur to Ahmedabad

- Delhi Mumbai Gondia Rath – Train No. 12215 - Depart time 14:25 – Arrival time 01:20 – Mon, Tue, Thus, Sat.

- Ashram Express – Train No. 12916 - Depart time 20:45 – Arrival time 07:40 – All days.
- Ahmendabad Shingaji Rajdhani - Train No. 12958 - Depart time 00:35 - Arrival time 10:05 – All days.
- Haridwar Ahmedabad Mail - Train No. 19106 - Depart time 04:55 – Arrival time 18:40 – All days.
- Aravali Express - Train No. 19708 - Depart time 08:30 – Arrival time 22:10 – All days.
- Delhi Porbandr Express - Train No. 19264 - Depart time 13:50 – Arrival time 02:55 – Mon, Thus.

Trains from Jaipur to Goa

- Maru Sagar Express – Train No. 12978 - Depart time 10:05 – Arrival time 13:15 – Fri.

Trains from Jaipur to Pune

- Jaipur Pune Settigunta Special – Train No. 09730 - Depart time 09:00 – Arrival time 08:05 – Sat.
- Jaipur Pune Settigunta Express – Train No. 12940 - Depart time 09:00 – Arrival time 08:05 – All days.

Trains from Jaipur to Alwar

- Ajmer Shatabdi Special – Train No. 04042 - Depart time 17:50 – Arrival time 19:39 – Wed.
- Ajmer Haridwar Special – Train No. 09640 - Depart time 21:50 – Arrival time 00:20 – Mon, Thus, Sat.
- Ajmer Shatabdi - Train No. 12016 - Depart time 17:50 - Arrival time 19:39 – All days except Wed.
- Delhi Garibrath - Train No. 12216 - Depart time 06:50 – Arrival time 09:14 – Mon, Wed, Thus, Sat.
- Mandor Express - Train No. 12462 - Depart time 00:50 – Arrival time 02:52 – All days.
- Ashram Express - Train No. 12915 - Depart time 04:30 – Arrival time 06:38– All days.

Trains from Jaipur to Bangalore

- Jaipur Mysore Express – Train No. 12976 - Depart time 19:40 – Arrival time 12:55 – Mon, Wed.

Trains from Jaipur to Bikaner

- Kota Hanumangarh Special – Train No. 09734 - Depart time 20:41 – Arrival time 04:30 – All days.
- Kolkata Jodhpur Express – Train No. 12307 - Depart time 01:00 – Arrival time 09:00 – All days.

- Rajsthan S Krant - Train No. 12463 - Depart time 03:25 - Arrival time 10:35 – Mon, Thus, Sat.
- Jaipur Bikaner Intercity - Train No. 12468 - Depart time 15:45 –Arrival time 22:40 – All days.
- Pratap Express - Train No. 12496 - Depart time 23:25 – Arrival time 07:20 – Sat.

Trains from Jaipur to Bhopal

- Jaipur Secunderbad S Fast Special – Train No. 09736 - Depart time 21:10 – Arrival time 09:40 – Sat.
- Jaipur Madras Express – Train No. 12968 - Depart time 19:40 – Arrival time 07:30 – Fri, Sat.
- Jaipur Mysore Express - Train No. 12976 - Depart time 19:40 - Arrival time 07:30 – Mon, Wed.
- Jodhpur Puri Express - Train No. 18474 - Depart time 19:40 –Arrival time 07:30 – Sat.
- Trains from Jaipur to Indore
- Jaipur Indore Settigunta Special – Train No. 09728 - Depart time 20:40 – Arrival time 06:35 – Tue.
- Intercity Express – Train No. 12466 - Depart time 10:55 – Arrival time 22:25 – All days.

- Jaipur Indore Express - Train No. 12974 - Depart time 21:10 - Arrival time 06:50 – Fri, Sat.

Trains from Jaipur to Chandigarh

- Jaipur Chandigarh Gondia Rath – Train No. 12983 - Depart time 20:05 – Arrival time 06:40 – Tue, Fri, Sun.

Trains from Jaipur to Hyderabad

- Jaipur Secunderbad S Fast Special – Train No. 09736 - Depart time 21:10 – Arrival time 03:55 – Sat.
- Jaipur Mysore Express - Train No. 12976 - Depart time 19:40 - Arrival time 23:45 – Mon, Wed.

Trains from Jaipur to Chennai

- Jaipur Madras Express – Train No. 12968 - Depart time 19:40 – Arrival time 09:45 – Fri, Sun.
- Jaipur Coimbatore Shrungavarpukta Express - Train No. 12970 - Depart time 19:40 - Arrival time 09:45 – Tue.

Trains from Jaipur to Lucknow

- Marudhar Express – Train No. 14854 - Depart time 15:40 – Arrival time 02:45 – Mon, Thus, Sat.

- Marudhar Express – Train No. 14864 - Depart time 15:40 – Arrival time 02:45 – Tue, Fri, Sun.
- Marudhar Express – Train No. 14866 - Depart time 15:40 – Arrival time 02:45 – Wed.
- Garib Nawaz Express – Train No. 15716 - Depart time 13:40 – Arrival time 05:25 – Mon.

Trains from Jaipur to Kolkata

- Jodhpur Kolkata Superfast – Train No. 12308 - Depart time 02:10 – Arrival time 04:00 – All days.
- Ananya Express – Train No. 12316 - Depart time 09:05 – Arrival time 15:10 – Monday
- Ajmer Sealdah Express – Train No. 12988 - Depart time 14:45 – Arrival time 15:55 – All days.
- Bikaner Kolkata Superfast – Train No. 22308 - Depart time 02:10 – Arrival time 04:00 – All days.

Trains from Jaipur to Surat

- Jaipur Pune Settigunta Special – Train No. 09730 - Depart time 09:00 – Arrival time 00:07 – Sat.
- Delhi Mumbai Gondia Rath – Train No. 12215 - Depart time 14:25 – Arrival time 04:43 – Mon, Tue, Thus, Sat.

- Jaipur Pune Settigunta Special – Train No. 12940 - Depart time 09:00 – Arrival time 00:07 – Tue.
- Jaipur Mumbai Superfast – Train No. 12956 - Depart time 14:10 – Arrival time 03:40 – All days.

Trains from Jaipur to Nagpur

- Jaipur Secunderabad Super-Fast Special – Train No. 09736 - Depart time 21:10 – Arrival time 16:40 – Sat.
- Madras Express – Train No. 12968 - Depart time 19:40 – Arrival time 14:00 – Fri, Sun.
- Jaipur Coimbatore Shrungavarpukta Express – Train No. 12970 - Depart time 19:40 – Arrival time 14:00 – Tue.
- Jodhpur Puri Express – Train No. 18474 - Depart time 19:40 – Arrival time 14:00 – Sat.

Trains from Kota to Jaipur

- Pune Jaipur Special – Train No. 09729 - Depart time 09:30 – Arrival time 13:40 – Mon.
- Kota Hanumangarh Special – Train No. 09734 - Depart time 16:40 – Arrival time 21:05 – All days.
- Dayodara Express – Train No. 12181 - Depart time 08:00 – Arrival time 11:55 – All days.

- Pune Jaipur Express – Train No. 12939 - Depart time 09:20 – Arrival time 13:40 – Thus.

The End

www.ingramcontent.com/pod-product-compliance
Lightning Source LLC
Chambersburg PA
CBHW031058080526
44587CB00011B/732